POWERFUL
According To
GOD

Henri,

Hope you enjoy this
book and that it will bless
your life.

Love
Nancy

POWERFUL
According To
GOD

A MONTH'S MEDITATION ON PRAYER
WITH WATCHMAN NEE

WATCHMAN NEE

CHRISTIAN FELLOWSHIP PUBLISHERS, INC.
NEW YORK

POWERFUL ACCORDING TO GOD

*A Month's Meditation on Prayer
with Watchman Nee*

Copyright © 2005
Christian Fellowship Publishers, Inc.
New York
All Right Reserved

ISBN 0-935008-85-3

Available from the Publishers at:

11515 ALLECINGIE PARKWAY
RICHMOND, VIRGINIA 23235
www.c-f-p.com

Printed in the United States of America

Forward

Prayer is the very breath of spiritual life. It begins with the sinner's prayer and it ends with the saint's final committing his spirit to God. It is so simple that a child can utter, yet it is so profound that it requires a lifetime to learn. There is no graduation from the school of prayer. Prayer measures the spirituality of a believer. It is the highest ministry one can ever render to God.

In this present volume brother Watchman Nee shares with us his thoughts on prayer so as to help us in our meditation. He leads us from why do we pray, through how should we pray, to how can we be powerful according to God in prayer. This spiritual art of prayer is open to all who have a heart for God.

Contents

Contents (*continued*)

A note to our readers:

The translation of the Chinese characters that appear on the cover and throughout this book is "Powerful According To God."

All Scripture quotations are from the American Standard Version of the Bible (1901), unless otherwise indicated.

PART ONE

Therefore Pray Ye

1

神前有能

Why Pray? A Mystery

"ASK, AND IT SHALL BE GIVEN YOU; SEEK, AND YE SHALL FIND;
KNOCK, AND IT SHALL BE OPENED UNTO YOU."
Matthew 7.7

Prayer is the most wonderful act in the spiritual realm as well as a most mysterious affair. Prayer is a mystery; and after we have considered a few questions on the subject I believe we will appreciate even more the mysterious character that surrounds prayer—for these are questions quite difficult to answer. Yet this observation is not meant to suggest that the mystery of prayer is incomprehensible or that the various problems concerning prayer are inexplicable. It is merely indicative of the fact that few people really know very much about them. In view of this, few are truly able to accomplish much for God in prayer. The power of prayer lies not in how much we pray but in how much our prayers are in accordance with the principle of prayer. Only prayers of this kind are of true value.

The foremost question to be asked is, Why pray? What is the use of praying? Is not God omniscient as well as omnipotent? Why must He wait till we pray before He commences to work? Since He knows, why must we tell Him everything

神前有能

(Philippians 4.6)? Being almighty, why does God not work directly? Why should He need our prayers? Why is it that only those who ask are given, only those who seek find, and only those who knock enter in (Matthew 7.7)? Why does God say: "Ye have not, because ye ask not" (James 4.2)?

Upon asking the above questions we must then continue to inquire as follows: Is prayer contrary to the will of God? What is the relationship between prayer and righteousness?

We know God never does anything against His own will. If opening doors is God's will, why should He wait until we knock before He opens? Why does He not simply open for us according to His own will without requiring us to knock? Being omniscient, God knows we need to have doors opened; why, then, must He wait for our knocking before He opens? If the door is to be opened and if opening doors is in accordance with God's will, and if furthermore He also knows that we need it to be opened, why does He wait for us to knock? Why does He not just open the door? What advantage does our knocking give to God?

Yet we must further ask these questions: Since God's will is to open the door and since opening the door is in accord with righteousness, will God nevertheless open the door if we do *not* knock? Or would He rather have His will and righteousness delayed without accomplishment in order to wait for our prayers? Will He really allow His will of opening doors to be restrained by our not knocking?

If so, will not the will of God be limited by us? Is God really almighty? If He is almighty, why can He not open the door all by Himself—why instead must He wait till we knock? Is God really able to accomplish His own will? But if He truly is able, then why is His opening of doors (God's will) governed by our knocking (man's prayer)?

By asking all these questions we come to realize that prayer is a great mystery. For here we see a principle of God's working, which is, that God's people must pray before God Himself will rise up and work: His will is only to be realized through the prayers of those who belong to Him: the prayers of the believers are to accomplish His will: God will not fulfill His will alone—He will perform only after His people show their sympathy in prayers.

Such being the case, it can therefore be said that prayer is none other than an act of the believer working together with God. Prayer is the union of the believer's thought with the will of God. The prayer which a believer utters on earth is but the voicing of the Lord's will in heaven. Prayer is not the expressing of our wish for God to yield to our petition and fill up our selfish desire. It is not a forcing of the Lord to change His will and perform what He is unwilling to do. No, prayer is simply speaking out the will of God through the mouth of the believer. Before God, the believer asks in prayer for the Lord's will to be done.

Prayer does not alter that which God has determined. It never changes anything; it merely achieves what He has already foreordained. Prayerlessness, though, *does* effect a change, because God will let many of His resolutions go suspended due to the lack from His people of prayerful cooperation with Him.

"Verily I say unto you, What things soever ye shall bind on earth shall be bound in heaven; and what things soever ye shall loose on earth shall be loosed in heaven" (Matthew 18.18). We are most familiar with this word of our Lord, yet it should be realized that this word has reference to prayer. And it is immediately followed by this statement of Christ's: "Again I say unto you, that if two of you shall agree on earth as touching anything that they shall ask, it shall be done for them of my Father who is in heaven" (v.19).

NOTES AND MEDITATIONS FROM:

DAY ONE – *Why Pray? A Mystery*

2

神前有能

To Whom Praying

"PRAY TO THY FATHER WHO IS IN SECRET, AND THY FATHER WHO
SEETH IN SECRET SHALL RECOMPENSE THEE."
Matthew 6.6

The prayers in the Bible are intelligent and not silly.
When the Lord Jesus teaches us to pray, His first
words are:"Our Father who art in heaven". He teaches us to pray to our Father in heaven, but we Christians
often pray to the God in our room. Our prayer should be
offered to the heavenly Father for Him to hear. God wants
us to send our prayers to heaven by faith, regardless if our
feeling be good or bad, or even if there be no feeling. If you
pray to, and expect to be heard by, the God in your room, I
am afraid you will receive many strange feelings and miracu-
lous experiences and visions from the God in your room.
These are given to you by Satan, and whatever you receive
from Satan belongs either to consciousness or sub-con-
sciousness.

Someone may not pray to the God in his room. He may
direct his prayers instead towards the person for whom he
prays. This too is most dangerous. Suppose you have a friend
who is over two thousand miles away from you. You pray for

2　　　　　　　　神前有能

him, asking God, as the case might be, to either revive him in the Word or to save him. Instead of directing your prayer towards God, you concentrate on your thought, your expectation, and your wish and send them out to your friend as a force (soul power). Your prayer is like a bow which shoots your thought, desire and wish as arrows towards your friend. He will be so oppressed by this force that he will do exactly what you have asked for. You may think your prayer is answered. But let me tell you, it is not God who answers your prayer, for you have not prayed to Him. It is merely an answer to a prayer which you directed towards your friend.

Someone claims his prayer is answered because, says he, "I have piled prayers on my friend." Indeed, for you prayed towards *him*, not towards God. Your prayer is answered, but not by God. Even though you do not know hypnosis, what you have secretly done has fulfilled the law of hypnotism. You have released your psychic force to perform this act.

Why is this so? Because you have not prayed to the God in heaven; instead your prayers are projected towards, piled upon, and laid siege to, the person for whom you pray. In appearance you are praying, but in actuality you are oppressing that person with your psychic power. If you use your soul force in praying for a certain one—say you pray that he

神前有能

2

should be at least disciplined if not punished—the prayer of your soul force will dart out at him and he will accordingly be sick. This is a fixed principle of the soul. It is as sure as the fact that a person will be scorched if he thrusts his finger into fire.

For this reason, we should not pray a prayer that asks that a person be punished if he does not do what is expected of him. Such prayer will cause him to suffer, and thus make the one who prayed such a prayer the instigator of his woe. If we pray, we should pray to God and not towards man. I personally have experienced the ill-effect of such prayer. Several years ago I was sick for over a year. This was due to the prayers of five or six persons being piled upon me. The more they prayed, the weaker I became. Finally I discovered the cause. I began to resist such prayers, asking God to disengage me from what they had prayed for. And so I got well.

NOTES AND MEDITATIONS FROM:
DAY TWO – *To Whom Praying*

神前有能

For Whom Do We Pray?

"AND THIS IS THE BOLDNESS WHICH WE HAVE TOWARDS HIM, THAT,
IF WE ASK ANYTHING ACCORDING TO HIS WILL, HE HEARETH US."
1 John 5.14

The first point to be noticed is that one who really prays is a person who not only often approaches God but also whose will frequently enters into God's will—that is to say, his thought often enters into God's thought. This is a most important principle in prayer.

There is a kind of prayer which originates entirely from our need. Though at times the Lord hears such prayers, He nonetheless gets little or nothing out of them. Please take note of this verse: "He gave them their request, but sent leanness into their soul" (Psalm 106.15). What does this passage mean? As Israel cried to God for the gratification of their lust, He did answer them by indeed giving them what they asked for—but with the result, however, of their being weakened before Him. Oh yes, sometimes God will hear and respond to your prayers for the sake of satisfying your own needs, yet His own will is not fulfilled. Let us see that such prayer does not have much value in it.

神前有能

But there is another kind of prayer, which comes out of God's own need. It is of God, and it is initiated by God. And such prayer is most valuable. In order to have such prayer, the one who prays must not only personally often appear before God but also he must allow his will to enter into God's will, his thought must be allowed to enter into God's thought. Since he habitually lives in the Lord's presence, such a person is given to know His will and thoughts. And these divine wills and thoughts quite naturally become his own desires, which he then expresses in prayer.

Oh how we must learn this second kind of prayer. Although we are immature and weak, we may nevertheless approach God and let His Spirit bring our will into God's will and our thought into God's thought. As we touch a little of His will and thought we come to understand a little more of how He works and what He requires of us. So that gradually the will and thought of God which we have known and entered into becomes in us our prayer. And such prayer is of great value.

Having entered into God's thought and thus having touched His will and purpose, Daniel found in his own heart the same desire as God's. The longing of God was reproduced in Daniel and became Daniel's desire. So that when he expressed this desire in prayer with cries and groanings, he

神前有能

was actually articulating God's desire. We need to have this kind of prayer, for it really touches the divine heart. We do not need more words; what we need is a touching more of the Lord's mind. Let the Spirit of God lead us into the intent of God's heart.

Of course, this kind of prayer will require time to learn. In the beginning of such a learning process let us not seek for more words nor for more thoughts. Our spirit should be calm and restful. We may bring our current situation to the Lord and consider it in the light of His countenance, or we may forget our present condition and simply meditate on His word before Him. Or we may just live before Him and try to touch Him with our spirit. As a matter of fact, it is not we who go forth to meet God but it is God who is waiting there for us. And there in His presence we perceive something and touch upon the will of God. The greatest wisdom comes, in fact, from this very source. By this, our will enters into His will and our thought enters into His heart. And from there our prayer will rise to Him.

As we bring our will and thought to God His own will and thought begin to be reproduced in us, and then this becomes our will and thought. This kind of prayer is most valuable and full of weight. Let us recall what the Lord Jesus said

about prayer: "After this manner therefore pray ye: Our
Father who art in heaven, hallowed be thy name. Thy kingdom come. Thy will be done, as in heaven, so on earth"
(Matthew 6.9,10). These are not just three phrases for us to
repeat. These words, which disclose the will and thought of
God, are to be reproduced in us when the Spirit of God
brings our mind to God. And as they become our will and
thought, the prayer which we afterwards utter is most valuable and most weighty.

God has many things to do on earth, touching many areas.
How, then, can we ever pray according to our own feeling
and thought? We should draw near to God and allow Him
to impress us with what He desires to do so that we ourselves may intercede with groanings. In case, as we approach
Him, God puts His will of spreading the gospel in us, this
soon will become a burden in us. And when we pray according to that burden, we shall have a sense as though our very
sigh is divulging the will of God. The Lord may put a variety
of wills or reproduce a variety of burdens in us. But whatever
be the particular will or burden, whenever it is reproduced in
a person's heart, that person is able to make the Lord's will
his own will and pray it out accordingly. When, in the case of
Daniel, he came before God, he touched a certain matter;
and then we saw that he prayed out that thing with deep

神前有能

groanings. How precious and substantial is prayer such as this. It can hallow God's name, bring in God's kingdom, and cause God's will to prevail on earth as in heaven.

NOTES AND MEDITATIONS FROM:
DAY THREE – *For Whom Do We Pray?*

4

When Ye Pray...
Be Not as the Hypocrites Nor as the Gentiles

"LET THE WORDS OF MY MOUTH AND THE MEDITATION OF MY HEART BE ACCEPTABLE IN THY SIGHT, O JEHOVAH, MY ROCK, AND MY REDEEMER."

Psalm 19.14

"And when ye pray," says the Lord, "ye shall not be as the hypocrites: for they love to stand and pray in the synagogues and in the corners of the streets, that they may be seen of men" (see Matthew 6.5-8). Prayer is primarily communion with God for the manifestation of God's glory. But these hypocrites use prayer which ought to glorify God to glorify themselves; consequently, they love to pray in the synagogues and in the corners of the streets. They act in this manner in order to be seen of men, since synagogues and street corners are obviously public places where people assemble. They do not pray to be heard of God, they pray instead to be seen of men. They purpose to manifest themselves. Such prayer is exceedingly superficial. It cannot be considered as praying to God nor communion with God. Since the motive of such kind of prayer is to receive glory from men, it has no registration with God, and therefore will

4　　　　神前有能

not obtain anything from Him. They have received their reward in the praise of men, hence they will not be remembered in the kingdom to come.

How, then, should we pray? The Lord continues: "But thou, when thou prayest, enter into thine inner chamber, and having shut thy door, pray to thy Father who is in secret, and thy Father who seeth in secret shall recompense thee." The phrase "inner chamber" is figurative here. Just as "synagogues" and "street corners" serve to represent exposed places, so "inner chamber" is representative of a hidden place. Brothers and sisters, you may indeed find an inner chamber even on street corners and in synagogues, on thoroughfare (highway) as well as in car. Why? Because an inner chamber is that place wherever you commune with God in secret, wherever you do not display your prayer on purpose. "Enter into thine inner chamber, and having shut thy door" means shutting out the world and shutting in yourselves. In other words, we are to disregard all outside voices and to quietly and singly (purely) pray to our God.

"Pray to thy Father who is in secret, and thy Father who seeth in secret shall recompense thee." How comforting is this word! Praying to your Father who is in secret requires faith. Although you do not sense anything in the open, you

神前有能　　　　　　　　　　　　4

believe you are praying to your Father who is in secret. He *is* in secret, beyond the observation of human eyes, yet He is also really there. He does not despise your prayer, He is there observing. All this is indicative of how much He is attentive to your prayer. He is not only observing, He is even going to recompense you. Can you believe this word?

When the Lord says "shall recompense", He *will* recompense. He is here guaranteeing that your prayer in secret shall not be in vain. If you really pray, He will surely recompense you. Even though there does not seem to be any recompense today, a day *shall* come when you will be rewarded. Brothers and sisters, is your prayer in secret able to stand the scrutiny of your Father who is in secret? Do you believe that the Father who is in secret shall recompense you?

The Lord not only teaches us not to display ourselves but also instructs us: "In praying use not vain repetitions, as the Gentiles do: for they think that they shall be heard for their much speaking." "Vain repetitions" in the Greek means uttering repetitious monotones in the way a stutterer would speak. In praying, the Gentiles repeat the same word monotonously. Such prayer is mere sound but with no meaning. As you stand nearby to listen to their prayer you will hear a monotonous, repetitive sound as though you were standing by a stream hearing the continuous rippling of water against the rocks or standing by a pebble-filled road and hearing the endless rolling of cart wheels passing over it. The Gentiles intone the same words many times. They think they shall be heard for their much speaking. Yet such prayer is vain and ineffective. We must not pray like that.

For this reason, let not the words of our prayers offered in a prayer meeting be void of meaning. When someone prays and you do not say amen, he will accuse you of not being of one mind. Yet if you do amen his prayer, he will use that word repetitiously. His prayer is not governed by the amount of heart but by the degree of supporting fervor. His prayer is not for the sake of discharging inward burden but to finish a speech. Many are the prayers effected by men, many are the utterances which far exceed the heart. I say again that such prayer is like the sound of rippling water against the rock or of cart wheels rolling endlessly over the pebble road. Such prayer has sound but no meaning. We should not pray like this.

"Be not therefore like unto them: for your Father knoweth what things ye have need of, before ye ask him." This verse shows us that whether or not our prayer is heard by God depends on our attitude before Him as well as our real need. It does not rest upon the much or the less of our words. If

神前有能

4

what we pray for is not what we need our prayer will go unanswered, however much word we may utter. Asking without need reveals greediness; it is asking amiss. God will gladly supply all our needs, but He is unwilling to gratify our selfish desire. How foolish for some people to say they need not pray since God knows all their needs. For the purpose of prayer is not to notify God but to express our trust, our faith, our expectation, and our heart desire. Hence we should pray. Yet in our praying, the desire of our heart should exceed the word of our lips, and faith should be stronger than word.

NOTES AND MEDITATIONS FROM:
DAY FOUR – *When Ye Pray...*

神前有能

"After This Manner Therefore Pray Ye" (1)

"HOLY FATHER, KEEP THEM IN THY NAME WHICH THOU HAST GIVEN ME, THAT THEY MAY BE ONE, EVEN AS WE ARE ONE."
John 17.11

"AFTER THIS MANNER THEREFORE PRAY YE. OUR FATHER WHO ART IN HEAVEN, HALLOWED BE THY NAME. THY KINGDOM COME. THY WILL BE DONE, AS IN HEAVEN, SO ON EARTH. GIVE US THIS DAY OUR DAILY BREAD. AND FORGIVE US OUR DEBTS, AS WE ALSO HAVE FORGIVEN OUR DEBTORS. AND BRING US NOT INTO TEMPTATION, BUT DELIVER US FROM THE EVIL ONE. FOR THINE IS THE KINGDOM, AND THE POWER, AND THE GLORY, FOR EVER. AMEN."
Matthew 6.9-13 margin

Now let us see how the Lord teaches us to pray. This prayer is commonly known as the Lord's prayer. Such a notion is wrong. For this is not the Lord's own prayer; it is the prayer He teaches us to pray. It is most distinctly stated in Luke 11.1-4. We should learn this prayer well.

"After this manner therefore pray ye." To pray like this does not mean to repeat these words each time we pray. No, the

5 神前有能

Lord does not mean that at all. He is teaching us how to pray, not asking us to repeat these words.

Ever since the world began, prayers have often been offered to God. Generation after generation, time after time, countless people have come to God and prayed. Seldom are there those who pray aright. Many think of what they themselves wish to have, few pay attention to what God wants. For this reason, the Lord Jesus opens His mouth to teach us to pray like this which we see here. And this kind of prayer is possessed of tremendous weight and greatness and depth. Now unless we have no intention to learn, we must learn to "pray like this" if we would learn how to pray at all. For God has come to earth to be a Man, and for the first time this Man tells us that only this kind of prayer is right to the point.

The Lord wants us to pray to "our Father who art in heaven." This name "Father" is a new way for men to address God. Formerly men called Him "the Almighty God", "the Most High God", "the everlasting God", or "Jehovah God"; none dared to call God "Father". Here for the very first time God is addressed as "Father". This plainly indicates that this prayer is offered by those who have been saved and have eternal life. Because men are saved, they can therefore call God "Father". Only those who are begotten of Him are the chil-

神前有能 5

dren of God. They alone can address God as "Father". This is
a prayer prayed to "our Father who art in heaven", and
hence it is offered up on the ground of being children. How
sweet and how comforting to come to God and to declare:
"Our Father who art in heaven."

Originally our Lord Jesus alone could call God "Father", but
now the Lord wants us also to call Him "our Father". Great
indeed is this revelation. Except for the fact that God so
loved us and gave His only begotten Son to us, how would
we ever be able to call Him "our Father"? Thank God,
through the death and resurrection of His Son, we now
become the children of God. We have obtained a new position. Hereafter our prayer is prayed to our Father who is in
heaven. How intimate, how free, and how exalted! May the
Spirit of the Lord give us greater understanding of God as
Father and also the confidence that our Father is both loving
and patient. He will not only hear our prayer but cause us to
have the joy of prayer as well.

The prayer which follows touches upon three areas which
concern the things of God—(a) "Hallowed be thy name"; (b)
"Thy kingdom come"; and (c) "Thy will be done, as in heav-
en, so on earth." This phrase—"as in heaven, so on earth"—
applies to all three of these things. It serves as a qualifier for

5 神前有能

all of them and is therefore not used exclusively to be only a part of the third statement that deals with the matter of God's "will." God's name is sanctified in the heavens; only on earth is it not being sanctified. In the heavens is the kingdom of God; only on earth is it missing. And the will of God is done in the heavens; yet only on this earth is His will not being obeyed. Accordingly, we need to pray.

The words in this so-called Lord's Prayer far exceed our thoughts. It would appear that ever since the creation of the world man has never come to God and prayed what He wants. The significance of this prayer lies in the fact that God Himself has come from behind the veil and told us what He desires. This is the first time God became man and told us the prayer that strikes the mark. Here we realize immediately what the kingdom of the heavens is, that it has been extended to include this earth. God calls us to pray what He desires, that which He considers to be essential.

神前有能

5

NOTES AND MEDITATIONS FROM:

DAY FIVE – *After This Manner Therefore Pray Ye (1)*

6

神前有能

"After This Manner Therefore Pray Ye" (2)

"BUT SEEK YE FIRST HIS KINGDOM, AND HIS RIGHTEOUSNESS; AND ALL THESE THINGS SHALL BE ADDED UNTO YOU."
Matthew 6.33

"AFTER THIS MANNER THEREFORE PRAY YE. OUR FATHER WHO ART IN HEAVEN, HALLOWED BE THY NAME. THY KINGDOM COME. THY WILL BE DONE, AS IN HEAVEN, SO ON EARTH. GIVE US THIS DAY OUR DAILY BREAD. AND FORGIVE US OUR DEBTS, AS WE ALSO HAVE FORGIVEN OUR DEBTORS. AND BRING US NOT INTO TEMPTATION, BUT DELIVER US FROM THE EVIL ONE. FOR THINE IS THE KINGDOM, AND THE POWER, AND THE GLORY, FOR EVER. AMEN."
Matthew 6.9-13 margin

The initial section of the so-called Lord's Prayer pertains to the three heart desires towards God.

The very first desire is "Hallowed be thy name". God has an expectation today, which is, that we pray that His name may be honored. His name is highly exalted among the angels,

神前有能

yet His name is abused carelessly by men. When His name is taken in vain by men He does not express His wrath by thundering from heaven. He instead hides Himself as though non-existent. He has never done anything against men for His name to be used in the vain manner that it is. But He will have His own children to pray: "Hallowed be thy name." If we love God and know Him, we will want His name to be honored. We shall feel hurt if people invoke His name in vain. Our desire will grow stronger and we will pray more earnestly: "Hallowed be thy name." Till one day, all will hallow this name, and none will dare to take His name in vain.

"Hallowed be thy name." God's name is not just a title which we use with our mouth to address Him; it is a great revelation which we receive from the Lord. God's name in the Bible is used to signify His own revelation to men in order that they may know Him. His name reveals His nature and manifests His perfection. This is not anything that the human soul can understand, it requires the Lord Himself to manifest it to us (see John 17.6). He says, "I made known unto them thy name, and will make it known; that the love wherewith thou lovedst me may be in them, and I in them" (John 17.26). To know God's name requires repeated revelations of the Lord.

神前有能 6

"Hallowed be thy name."This not only is our heart desire
but also constitutes our worship to the Father. We ought to
give glory to God. We should commence our prayer with
praise. Before we anticipate His mercy and grace, let us glorify God. Let Him receive the praise due His perfectness; and
then shall we receive grace from Him. The preeminent and
the ultimate of our prayer is that God may get glory.

"Hallowed be thy name." God's name is linked with His
glory. "I had regard for my holy name, which the house of
Israel had profaned among the nations, whither they went"
(Ezekiel 36.21). The people of Israel had not hallowed God's
name, they had instead profaned that name wherever they
went. Yet God had regard for His holy name. Our Lord
requires of us this holy desire. In other words, He wishes to
glorify God's name through us. The name of God must first
be hallowed in each individual heart, and then this our
desire will be deepened. The cross must do a deeper work in
us before we can glorify God's name. Otherwise we cannot
view it as a holy desire but only a whimsical fancy. This
being the case, what dealing and purification we need to
receive in our lives!

The second desire is "Thy kingdom come". What kind of a kingdom is this? Judging from the context, this has reference to

6

神前有能

the kingdom of the heavens. In teaching us to pray "Thy kingdom come", the Lord is saying that there is the kingdom of God in heaven, but that on this earth there is not, and that therefore we ought to pray to God to extend the boundary of the kingdom of the heavens to reach to this earth. The kingdom of God in the Bible is spoken of in geographical as well as in historical terms. History is a matter of time, whereas geography is a matter of space.

According to the Scriptures, the geographical factor of the kingdom of God exceeds its historical factor. "If I by the Spirit of God cast out demons," said the Lord Jesus, "then is the kingdom of God come upon you" (Matthew 12.28). Is this a historical problem? No, it is a geographical problem. Wherever the Son of God casts out demons by the Spirit of God, there is the kingdom of God. So during this period of time, the kingdom of God is more geographical than historical.

"Thy kingdom come"! This is not only a *desire* of the church, it is also a *responsibility* of the church. The church ought to bring the kingdom of God to earth. In order to accomplish this task the church must be willing to pay any price, submitting herself to the restraint and control of heaven that she may be the outlet of heaven, letting through the authority of heaven onto earth. If the church is to bring in the king-

神前有能　　　　　　　　6

dom of God she must not be ignorant of the devices of
Satan (see 2 Corinthians 2.11) and she needs to be clothed
with the whole armor of God that she may be able to stand
against the wiles of the devil (Ephesians 6.11). Wherever the
kingdom of God comes down, the demons will be driven out
of that place. When the kingdom of God rules over the earth
completely, Satan will be cast into the bottomless pit (see
Revelation 20.1-3).

The third desire is "Thy will be done, as in heaven, so on earth".
This reveals that the will of God is done in heaven, but that
on earth it is not wholly done. He is God; who can hinder
His will from being done? Is it man who hinders God or is it
Satan? Actually none can hinder Him. Then why such a
prayer? In order to answer this question we need to be clear
on the principle of prayer.

Throughout the entire Bible are to be found a number of
basic principles of truth, among which is the principle of
prayer. Now let us immediately recognize that the very fact
that prayer is found in the Bible is most amazing. We learn in
the Scriptures, do we not, that God knows beforehand what
we need. Then why should we pray at all? For since God is
omniscient, then according to human logic there is really no
need for men to pray! Yet this is the amazing thing about the

6 神前有能

Bible; that it tells how God wants men to pray! Prayer is this: that God desires to do a certain thing, yet He will not do it alone; He waits until men on earth so pray, and only then will He do it. He has His own will and mind, nevertheless He waits for men to pray. Not that God does not know our need, but that He will supply our need only after we have prayed. He will not move till somebody prays.

神前有能

6

NOTES AND MEDITATIONS FROM:

DAY SIX – *After This Manner Therefore Pray Ye (2)*

7

神前有能

"After This Manner Therefore Pray Ye" (3)

"JEHOVAH IS MY SHEPHERD; I SHALL NOT WANT."
Psalm 23.1

"AFTER THIS MANNER THEREFORE PRAY YE. OUR FATHER WHO ART IN HEAVEN, HALLOWED BE THY NAME. THY KINGDOM COME. THY WILL BE DONE, AS IN HEAVEN, SO ON EARTH. GIVE US THIS DAY OUR DAILY BREAD. AND FORGIVE US OUR DEBTS, AS WE ALSO HAVE FORGIVEN OUR DEBTORS. AND BRING US NOT INTO TEMPTATION, BUT DELIVER US FROM THE EVIL ONE. FOR THINE IS THE KINGDOM, AND THE POWER, AND THE GLORY, FOR EVER. AMEN."
Matthew 6.9-13 margin

In the second section of Jesus' teaching on prayer, we have three requests for ourselves.

We first of all read: "Give us this day our daily bread." Some people have trouble in understanding how the Lord can teach us to pray for God's name, God's kingdom, and God's will, but then suddenly turn to the matter of daily bread. The plunge in prayer from such sublime heights to such a mundane level seems like a sudden descent of ten thousand feet. But let us recognize that there is a very good reason for it.

The Lord takes note of the person who truly belongs to God and prays constantly for the name, kingdom, and will of God. Since such prayer is so essential, the one who prays will invariably draw down upon him the assault of Satan. There is therefore one matter which needs to be prayed for—daily bread. Food is man's immediate need; it is a great temptation. When a person's daily bread becomes a problem, this constitutes an exceedingly great temptation. On the one hand, you desire that God's name be hallowed and you pray that His kingdom will come and His will be done on earth; on the other hand, you as a person still live on earth and have need of daily bread. Satan knows about this necessity of yours. And hence you must exercise this protective prayer. This is a Christian's prayer for himself, asking the Lord for protection. Otherwise, while he prays such transcendental (heavenly) prayer he will be attacked by the enemy. Satan can assault us in this area. If we are in need of daily bread and are assaulted in this regard, our prayer will be affected. May we see the necessity of this prayer. As long as we are still on earth as human beings our bodies have this need of daily food. Consequently, we must ask God to give us our daily bread.

神前有能 7

This prayer also shows us how we need to look to God daily and to pray to Him daily. For so the Lord teaches us here, saying, "Give us *this day* our daily bread." It is not praying weekly, but rather daily. We have nothing to lean upon on earth, nor do we have any savings. We have to request our daily bread for *today*—not for a week's or a month's supply. How we must rely on God! Here we see that our Lord is not unmindful of our daily bread, neither does He teach us not to ask, but He wants us to ask daily.

Now as a matter of fact our Father knows already the things which we need. Yet the Lord here wants us to pray to God every day for our daily bread because the Lord longs that we learn to look to the Father daily, thus exercising our faith from day to day. How often we become anxious for too far ahead and so we pray for remote needs. This we should not do. Let us realize that if we have a strong desire for God's name and kingdom and will, our trouble will automatically become great. But since God gives us *this day* our daily bread, we can pray for our tomorrow's bread when tomorrow comes. "Therefore do not be anxious about tomorrow, for tomorrow will be anxious for itself. Let the day's own trouble be sufficient for the day" (Matthew 6.34 RSV).

The second request is: "Forgive us our debts, as we also have forgiven our debtors." We have the request for physical need on the one hand and the request for a conscience without offense on the other. Day by day we cannot avoid offending God in many areas. Though these may not all be sins, they nonetheless can be debts. What should be done and has not been done is debt; what should be said and has not been said is also debt. Hence it is not very easy to maintain a conscience void of offense before God. Each night before retiring we discover that many things have happened during the day which are offensive to God. These may not necessarily be sins, nevertheless they are debts. As we ask God to forgive our debts and to remember them no more we are able to have a conscience without offense. This is extremely important. Having our debts as well as our sins forgiven, we now have a clear conscience to live with boldness before God.

We ask God to forgive our debts as we also have forgiven our debtors. If a person is hard bargaining towards his brothers and sisters and cannot forget their offenses towards him, he is not qualified to ask God to forgive his debts. He whose heart is so narrow as to always notice how people have hurt and offended him is unable to pray such a prayer before God. We need to have a forgiving heart before we can come to the Father with boldness, asking Him to "forgive us our debts as we also have forgiven our debtors." We cannot

神前有能

ask God to forgive our debts if we have not also forgiven another's debts. How can we open our mouths to ask for God's forgiveness unless we have first forgiven our debtors?

Here may we notice this one thing, that besides telling us of our relationship with the Father, the Bible also shows us our relationship among brothers and sisters. A brother or a sister deceives himself or herself if he or she considers himself or herself as right with God because he or she remembers the relationship with God although neglecting the relationship with other brothers and sisters. If we have this day created a discord with any brother or sister, we instantly lose the blessing of God. Likewise too, we incur a debt—though not a sin—if we today fail to do or to say what we ought to our brothers and sisters. Let us not fancy (imagine) that as long as there is not sin everything is fine; we must also not have any debt. If we can neither forgive nor forget whatever griev-ances we have against our brothers or sisters, this will hinder us from receiving God's forgiveness. Just as we treat brothers and sisters, so God will also treat us. It is a serious self-deception if we reckon God has forgiven our debts to Him while simultaneously we continue to remember our debtors, counting and complaining all the time. For the Lord explicit-ly teaches us to pray: "Forgive us our debts, as we also have forgiven our debtors."

Please notice the words "As . . . forgiven". Without "forgiven", how can there be "as"? If you have not forgiven your debtors, your debts will still be remembered by God. In case you *have* forgiven your debtors from your heart and have allowed these debts to pass completely away as though there were nothing, you can then come to God with boldness, saying, "Forgive me my debts as I also have forgiven my debtors." And the result is that God cannot but forgive your debts. Do let us happily fulfill "forgive our debtors", lest the lack thereof affect our own forgiveness before God.

And the third request? "*Bring us not into temptation, but deliver us from the evil one.*" The first request pertains to our physical need; the second request is concerned with our relationship with brothers and sisters; this final one speaks of our relation with Satan. "Bring us not into temptation" is the negative side, whereas "deliver us from the evil one" is the positive. As we live on earth for God with a strong heart desire for His name, His kingdom, and His will, we on the one hand will have physical need for which we must look to God to supply our daily bread, and on the other hand will experience the need of a conscience to be ever clean and blameless before God and for which we must ask Him to forgive us our debts. Yet there is another need we encounter—the need to have peace, for the sake of which we ask God to deliver

神前有能

us from the hand of Satan.

Brothers and sisters, the more we walk in the way of the kingdom of the heavens, the stronger will be our temptations. How should we cope with the situation? We should pray, asking God: "Bring us not into temptation." Never be so self-confident as to dare to face any temptation. Since the Lord has taught us thus to pray, we ought to ask God not to lead us into temptation. We do not know when temptation will come, but we can pray beforehand that God will not bring us into it.

Such prayer is for the sake of protection. Instead of waiting daily for temptation to come upon us, we should daily pray that the Lord will not bring us into it. Only whatever is permitted by the Lord may come to us; but what He does not permit, we ask that it may not happen to us. Otherwise, we will be so occupied with fighting against temptation from dawn to dusk that we can do nothing else. We must ask the Lord to not lead us into temptation, so that we may neither meet those whom we should not meet nor encounter the things which should not happen to us. This is a kind of protective prayer. And we ought to pray to God for this protection, asking Him to give us our daily bread, to solve our problem of a clean conscience, and to not bring us into temptation.

7　　　　　神前有能

We should not only ask the Lord: "Bring us not into temptation" but also: "Deliver us from the evil one." This latter side is a positive request. No matter where the hand of Satan is—whether it pertains to our daily bread or to his accusing our conscience or to whatever temptation with which he may tempt us—we ask the Lord to deliver us from the evil one. In other words, we do not expect to fall into the hand of the evil one in anything. By reading Matthew 8 and 9 we may realize that the hand of Satan is on more things than we assume. With respect to the human body, his hand may be in terms of a high fever; with respect to the sea, a sudden storm. His hand may show itself through demon possession in the case of man or through drowning in the case of a herd of swine. It may also be reflected in rejection of, or opposition to, the Lord in human hearts without cause. In any event, Satan is out to hurt people and to cause them to suffer. We should therefore pray, asking the Lord to deliver us from the evil one.

神前有能

NOTES AND MEDITATIONS FROM:

DAY SEVEN – *After This Manner Therefore Pray Ye* (3)

神前有能

"After This Manner Therefore Pray Ye" (4)

"BLESS JEHOVAH, O MY SOUL; AND ALL THAT IS WITHIN ME, BLESS HIS HOLY NAME."

Psalm 103.1

"AFTER THIS MANNER THEREFORE PRAY YE. OUR FATHER WHO ART IN HEAVEN, HALLOWED BE THY NAME. THY KINGDOM COME. THY WILL BE DONE, AS IN HEAVEN, SO ON EARTH. GIVE US THIS DAY OUR DAILY BREAD. AND FORGIVE US OUR DEBTS, AS WE ALSO HAVE FORGIVEN OUR DEBTORS. AND BRING US NOT INTO TEMPTATION, BUT DELIVER US FROM THE EVIL ONE. FOR THINE IS THE KINGDOM, AND THE POWER, AND THE GLORY, FOR EVER. AMEN."

Matthew 6.9-13 margin

Finally, the Lord teaches us to praise God for three things: *"For thine is the kingdom, and the power, and the glory, for ever. Amen."* Such praises declare that the kingdom is the Father's, the power is the Father's, and the glory is the Father's. These three matters to be praised are related to the deliverance from the evil one; yea, even more so, they are related to the whole prayer which our Lord has taught. The reason for asking to be delivered from the evil one is because the kingdom is the Father's, not Satan's; because the power is the Father's, not Satan's; and because the glory is the Father's, not Satan's. The emphasis is right here: that since the kingdom is the Father's, we ought not fall into Satan's hand; and that since the power is the Father's, we must not fall into Satan's hand; and that again, since the glory is the Father's, we shall not fall into Satan's hand. This constitutes a very strong reason. If we fall into Satan's hand, how can the Father be glorified? But if it is the Father who rules, then Satan has no power over us. The kingdom of the heavens belongs to the Father, therefore we cannot and we should not fall into the hand of Satan.

Concerning power, we ought to remember the words our Lord has said to us: "Behold, I have given you authority to tread upon serpents and scorpions, and over all the power of the enemy; and nothing shall in any wise hurt you" (Luke 10.19). The authority which the Lord says He has given overcomes all the power of the enemy. For there is power in that authority. The Lord wishes us to know that in the kingdom there is an authority, and behind that authority is the power which is all-controlling. The kingdom is God's, not Satan's; naturally the authority is also God's, not Satan's; and the power too is God's, not Satan's. And as to glory, it likewise belongs to God and not to Satan. The kingdom and power and glory being all

God's, those who belong to Him can expect to be delivered from temptation and from the hand of Satan. In the New Testament the name of the Lord usually represents authority, while the Holy Spirit represents power. All authority is in the name of the Lord; all power is in the Holy Spirit. The kingdom speaks of the rule of heaven, hence it is God's authority. The Holy Spirit is the power by which God acts. Since the kingdom is God's, Satan has nowhere to rule; since the power is the Holy Spirit, the adversary has no means by which to compete. We are told in Matthew 12.28 that as soon as the demons meet the Holy Spirit they are immediately cast out. And finally, the glory is also God's. Hence we may loudly declare and highly praise: "Thine is the kingdom, and the power, and the glory, for ever. Amen."

The Lord teaches us to pray after this manner. This is not to recite it as a formality, but rather to pray according to the principle revealed by this prayer. This should form the basis for all prayers. For the sake of God, we earnestly desire that His name be hallowed, His kingdom come, and His will be done on earth as in heaven. Likewise, too, for the sake of the fact that the kingdom and power and glory are God's, we give Him all the praises. Since the kingdom and power and glory are all His, God's name ought to be hallowed, His kingdom ought to come, and His will ought to be done on

神前有能

earth as in heaven. Since the kingdom and power and glory are His, we should pray to Him for our daily bread, for the forgiveness of our debts, and for deliverance from temptation and the evil one. All our prayers should be modeled after this one.

Some people have insinuated that this prayer is not given to us Christians because it does not conclude with "in the name of the Lord". Such insinuation is plain folly (absurdity). Because the prayer which the Lord teaches us here is not a form prayer. Moreover, we wonder which prayer in the New Testament ends with the words "in the name of the Lord". When, for instance, the disciples cried to the Lord in the boat, saying, "Save, Lord; we perish" (Matthew 8.25), were there such words as "in the name of the Lord" included? It is clear that the Lord is not teaching us to say the exact words; rather, He wants us to pray according to the principle He hereby gives. He enumerates (specifies) the various elements we should pray for, without telling us to repeat these very words.

神前有能 8

NOTES AND MEDITATIONS FROM:

DAY EIGHT – *After This Manner Therefore Pray Ye* (4)

PART TWO

When Ye Pray

9

神前有能

Prayer is Righteousness

"FOR THE KINGDOM OF GOD IS NOT EATING AND DRINKING, BUT RIGHTEOUSNESS AND PEACE AND JOY IN THE HOLY SPIRIT."
Romans 14.17

Three things are mentioned in Matthew 6.1-18: (1) alms (charity), (2) prayer, and (3) fasting. Verse 1 warns: "Take heed that ye do not your righteousness before men." This is the general theme. Verses 2-4 deal with alms; 5-15, with prayer; and 16-18, with fasting. All three are forms of righteousness. Giving alms is visible and is related to other men. Prayer is related to God, and fasting is related to one's self. Regardless of whether towards men, God or self, none of them must be done with the purpose of having such righteousness seen by men. Alms, prayer and fasting will all be rewarded, but if they are seen by men, the future reward is canceled. Christians should cultivate the habit of doing these righteousnesses secretly. As they practice righteousness, they need to avoid the temptation of two extremes. One is to do all of these things before men and to be influenced by men. The other is to do all according to one's own idea without any consideration of men. Both these extremes are unacceptable.

The second righteousness that needs to be practiced in secret is prayer. Prayer is for the manifestation of the glory of God as well as to acknowledge our own inadequacy. This is why we seek after God. Yet how sad that men will take advantage of glorifying God to glorify themselves. They pray to be heard of men. The hypocrites pray in the synagogues and on the streets with the intention of being seen by men. But in so doing, they have received their reward: they have received it from men. The Lord does not speak here of the answer of prayer, but of the reward of prayer, for it is in the same category as the reward of fasting mentioned below. Hence, the reward of prayer does not refer to the answer of prayer. It is a recompense according to works. Prayer, therefore, has not only answer today but also reward in the future at the judgment seat of Christ. It will be remembered at the judgment seat as a righteousness that is to be rewarded. So that whoever prays to be heard of men now will have no possibility of being rewarded then at the judgment seat.

Prayer is a kind of righteousness. I hope that brothers and sisters will not be lacking in such righteousness. He who does not pray will receive no answer today and no reward in the future. In reality, prayer is our intimate communion with God. If anyone uses it as a means to be seen by men, he is a very shallow person. It should instead be our greatest secret. The

Lord shows us that when we pray we should enter an inner chamber (synagogues, corners of the streets, and inner chamber are all symbolisms in this passage). An inner chamber has reference to a secret place where no one can purposely show off his prayer. To "shut thy door" is to shut out all that is of the world and to shut oneself in so as not even to be able to answer the doorbell. It leaves the person alone with God in prayer. It is a righteousness as well as a reason for God to reward us. This must be something which greatly pleases Him. So that the purpose of prayer is more than receiving answer, it also involves future reward. "Pray to thy Father who is in secret, and thy Father who seeth in secret shall recompense thee." Our Father watches our every action.

Alms are to be done in secret; but prayer is not only something to be done in secret but is also something in which we must be careful as to our words. Thus prayer is a greater form of righteousness than alms-giving. The Lord has to continue further in teaching us how to pray. Prayer must not only be in secret, it must also be devoid of vain repetitions such as the Gentiles are guilty of voicing. Prayer should be simple. "Vain repetitions" in the Greek language conveys a sense of the sound of water running through stones: it makes the same sound all the time. Its sound is monotonous and repetitious. Also, "much speaking" is a phrase which in the Greek points to the sound of a wheel rolling over stones. Thus the Lord uses these two expressions to describe the sound of prayer. It is like water slapping against stones and a wheel rolling over stones. They are totally meaningless. Hence in our praying, let it not be seen by men nor be done in the form of much meaningless speaking.

In public prayer, we are more or less affected by men. We not only pray to God but also pray to be heard by men. Our heart is not able to concentrate wholly on God. Some may not be able to stop praying because of the amens said by the brethren. Thus their prayer is not measured by the depth of their heart desire but by the number of amens elicited from the brethren. This nullifies the effectiveness of prayer. Prayer must be measured by heart desire; it should never exceed heart desire. Let us not quit praying in the meeting; but by the same token, let us not pray only in the meeting. Pray not only in public, pray also in private. If the words in your secret prayer are simple, then do not let them be far different in your open prayer. There is no need for much speaking, "for your Father knoweth what things ye have need of, before ye ask him." The answer to your prayer is according to your heart desire and attitude of prayer, not according to your words. Do not try to force God, for He already knows what you need. Then, why pray? It is that I may express my attitude of willingness to believe and depend on Him.

神前有能

9

NOTES AND MEDITATIONS FROM:

DAY NINE – *Prayer is Righteousness*

10 神前有能

Pray in the Name of the Lord Jesus

"IF YE SHALL ASK ANYTHING IN MY NAME, THAT WILL I DO."
John 14.14

The name of the Lord Jesus is very special. It is something which Christ did not possess while on earth. When He was on earth His name was Jesus. This is what Matthew 1 tells us. But in Philippians 2 it is further indicated that the Lord having humbled Himself unto death—even the death of the cross—God has also highly exalted Him and given Him a name which is above every name. What is this name? Let us read Philippians 2.10-11— "That in the name of Jesus every knee should bow, of things in heaven and things on earth and things under the earth, and that every tongue should confess that Jesus Christ is Lord, to the glory of God the Father." This name is "the name of Jesus". Was He not called Jesus while on earth? Yet this is a name given Him after He had ascended to heaven. Because of His obedience to God even unto death—and that the death of the cross—the Lord is exalted and given a name which is above every name. And that name above every name is the name of Jesus.

10

神前有能

It is not only Paul who, having received revelation, says that the name of the Lord Jesus has undergone this great change; even the Lord Jesus Himself shows us that His name has undergone a drastic change: "Hitherto have ye asked nothing in my name: ask, and ye shall receive, that your joy may be made full. . . . In that day ye shall ask in my name" (John 16.24, 26a). "In that day", says Jesus, not today; but just wait until that day and then you shall ask in My name. On the day He spoke these words He had not yet had this name that is above all names. But He receives that name above all names "in that day", and "in that day" we can go to the Father and ask in His name.

May God open our eyes to see that after His ascension the name of the Lord Jesus has undergone a great change—a change which is beyond the comprehension of our mind. That name is a God-given name; that name is above all names.

What does that name represent? It represents authority as well as power. Why does it represent authority and power? "That in the name of Jesus every knee should bow, of things in heaven and things on earth and things under the earth, and that every tongue should confess that Jesus Christ is Lord, to the glory of God the Father"—this is authority.

神前有能 10

Whoever he is, he should bow in the name of Jesus; whoever he is, he should confess that Jesus is Lord. For this reason the name of Jesus means that God has given Him an authority and power which exceeds all.

During His last night on earth with the disciples the Lord Jesus said to them: "Whatsoever ye shall ask in my name, that will I do, that the Father may be glorified in the Son" (John 14.13). He entrusted them with something of tremendous value; He gave His name to them. His name is authority; there is nothing greater than what He has given us. Just imagine what will happen if we adversely use the name which the Lord Jesus has committed to us. Here, for example, is a man who holds great power. Each time he gives an order it becomes effective if he puts his seal on it. Suppose he gives his seal to another person. He will have to be responsible for whatever order this other man issues that has his seal attached to it. Do you think he will carelessly entrust his seal to just any person? Of course not. Yet the Lord Jesus has committed His name to us. The name of the Lord Jesus is above all names. He is nevertheless willing to entrust His name to us. Do we truly appreciate what responsibility He has taken upon Himself in giving His name to us? And whatever we do in His name, that will God bear responsibility for. This is indeed tremendous! That whatever is done in the name of the Lord Jesus God will be responsible for!

Do we realize that here is a name which is both authority and power which is put into the hand of the church to be used? The church ought to use the name of the Lord wisely. We sometimes say that the church does rule, but how can she rule without having the name? She holds the keys of the kingdom and is responsible to bring in the kingdom; yet without this name she is unable to open up the kingdom. The purpose of God is indeed to swallow death by life in the church and to bind Satan through the church; but except we have this name and know how to use it, we will not be able to fulfill our mission. We must consequently see that this name is given by the Lord Jesus to the church.

神前有能

10

NOTES AND MEDITATIONS FROM:

DAY TEN – *Pray in the Name of the Lord Jesus*

11

神前有能

Pray in Faith

"ALL THINGS WHATSOEVER YE PRAY AND ASK FOR, BELIEVE THAT YE
RECEIVE THEM, AND YE SHALL HAVE THEM."
Mark 11.24

The prayer life of new believers is mainly involved with
conscience and faith. Though prayer is rather profound, to new believers it is only a matter of conscience and faith. If their conscience before God is without
offense, their faith can easily be strong. And if their faith is
sufficiently strong, their prayer will easily be answered.
Therefore it is necessary for them to have faith.

What is faith? It is not doubting in prayer. It is God who
constrains us to pray. It is God who promises that we may
pray to Him. He cannot but answer if we pray. He says:
"Knock and it shall be opened unto you." How can I knock
and He refuse to open? He says: "Seek and ye shall find."
Can I seek and find not? He says: "Ask and it shall be given
you." It is absolutely impossible for me to ask and not be
given. Who do we think our God is? We ought to see how
faithful and dependable are the promises of God.

We may have believed in the Lord for some years now, but

11 神前有能

can recall that at one time it was quite difficult to believe, for faith is based on the knowledge of God. The depth of our knowledge of God measures the depth of our faith. We need to know God more that we may have more faith. Salvation is based on knowing. Now that we have been saved, have known God, we can believe without any difficulty. If we believe, God will answer us. Let us learn from the beginning to be people full of faith. Do not live by feelings nor by thoughts; learn to live by faith. As we learn to believe in God, we shall find our prayers answered.

Faith comes by the Word of God. For God's Word is like cash that can be taken and used. God's promise is God's work. Promise tells us what God's work is, and work manifests to us the promise of God. If we believe the Word of God and do not doubt, we will abide in faith and see how trustworthy is all that God has said. Our prayers shall be answered.

There is yet a positive condition that must be fulfilled, and that is, one must believe. Otherwise prayer will not be effectual. The incident in Mark 11.12-24 shows us clearly the necessity of faith in prayer. The Lord with His disciples came out from Bethany. He hungered on the way. Seeing a fig tree afar off, He approached that He might find some figs, but He found nothing except leaves. So He cursed the tree, saying,

神前有能

11

"No man eat fruit from thee henceforward for ever." The next morning they passed by and saw the fig tree withered away from the roots. The disciples were astonished. And the Lord answered, "Have faith in God. Verily I say unto you, Whosoever shall say unto this mountain, Be thou taken up and cast into the sea; and shall not doubt in his heart, but shall believe that what he saith cometh to pass; he shall have it. Therefore I say unto you, All things whatsoever ye pray and ask for, believe that ye receive them, and ye shall have them."

One must believe when he is praying, because if he believes then he shall receive. What is faith? Faith is believing that he receives what he prays for.

We Christians often have a wrong concept of faith. The Lord says, he who believes that he *receives* shall receive; but we Christians maintain, he who believes that he *will receive* shall have it. Thus we have here two different kinds of faith. The Lord uses the word "receive" twice (Chinese version): once "he receives," then he "shall receive." Many believers, however, fasten their faith to "shall receive." We pray to the Lord, believing that we *shall* receive what we ask. We believe the mountain *will* be removed to the sea. Great seems to be our faith. But we have disassociated faith from "he receives" to he "shall receive." This is not the kind of faith our Lord is talk-

11　　　　　神前有能

ing about. The faith of which Scripture speaks is associated with "he receives." It is far more exact than "shall receive."

So, what is faith? Faith is when you are brought to the place whereby you can claim God has already heard your prayer. It is not when you say God will hear you. You kneel down to pray, and somehow you are able to say: Thank God, He has heard my prayer. Thank God, this is done. Now, this is faith, for it adheres to "he receives." If you rise from your knees and proclaim that you believe God will hear you or God must hear you, however insistent you are, nothing will happen. Your decision does not produce any result.

The Lord says, "Believe that ye receive them, and ye shall have them." He did not say: "Believe that ye will receive them, and ye shall have them." Brethren, do you get the key? True faith knows "it is done" already. Thank God, for He has heard my prayer.

神前有能

11

NOTES AND MEDITATIONS FROM:

DAY ELEVEN – *Pray in Faith*

12

Prayer and Burden

"CAST THY BURDEN UPON JEHOVAH, AND HE WILL SUSTAIN THEE."
Psalm 55.22a

Each time God puts a prayer thought into us His Holy Spirit first moves us into having a burden to pray for that particular matter. As soon as we receive such feeling we should immediately give ourselves to prayer. We should pay the cost of praying well for this matter. For when we are moved by the Holy Spirit our own spirit instantly senses a burden as though something were being laid upon our heart. After we pray it out we feel relieved as though having a heavy stone removed from off us. But in case we do not pour it out in prayer, we will get the feeling of something not yet done. If we do not pray it out we are not in harmony with God's heart. Were we to be faithful in prayer, that is to say, were we to pray as soon as the burden comes upon us, prayer would not become a weight, it would instead be light and pleasant.

What a pity that so many people quench the Holy Spirit here. They quench the sensation which the Holy Spirit gives to move them to pray. Hereafter, few of such sensations will

神前有能

ever come upon them. Thus they are no longer useful vessels before the Lord. The Lord can achieve nothing through them since they are no longer able to breathe out in prayer the will of God. Oh, if ever we fall to such an extent of having no prayer burden, we will have sunk indeed into a most perilous situation, for we have already lost communion with God and He is no more able to use us in His work. For this reason, we must be extra careful in dealing with the feeling which the Holy Spirit gives to us. Whenever there is a prayer burden we should immediately inquire of the Lord, saying, "O God, what do you want me to pray for? What is it which you wish to accomplish that needs me to pray?" And were we to pray it out, we would be entrusted by God with the next prayer. If our first burden is not yet discharged, we are unable to take up the second load.

Let us ask the Lord to make us faithful prayer partners. As soon as the burden comes, we have it discharged by praying it out. If the burden grows too heavy and it cannot be discharged by prayer, then we should fast. When prayer cannot discharge a burden, fasting must follow. Through fasting, the burden of prayer may quickly be discharged, since fasting is able to help us discharge the heaviest of burdens.

If anyone should continue on in performing the work of

神前有能

12

prayer, he will become a channel for the will of God. Whenever the Lord has anything to do, He will seek that person out. Let me say this, that the will of God is always in search of a way out. The Lord is always apprehending someone or some people to be the expression of His will. If many will rise up to do this work, He will do many things because of their prayers.

In order to fulfill the ministry of prayer we must have a burden for prayer before God. We do not intend to set up a law; we only wish to present this principle here. Let us recognize this one thing: burden is the secret of prayer. If a person does not feel within him burden to pray for a particular matter he can hardly succeed in prayer. In a prayer meeting some brothers and sisters may mention a great many subjects for prayer. But if you are not touched inwardly, you cannot pray. Therefore every brother and sister who comes to a prayer meeting ought to have prayer burden so as to pray.

At the same time do not be totally absorbed in only considering what burden you yourself have; you should also sense the burdens of other brothers and sisters in the meeting. For example, one sister may be troubled by her husband; one brother may be sick. If in a prayer meeting one person asks God to save the sister's husband, and this is followed by

12　　　　神前有能

another person who asks God to heal the brother's sickness, and in turn this is followed by still another individual who remembers before God something else, then each person is only praying for his own particular matter. Such prayer is not in accordance with the principle of praying thrice (see Day Fifteen). For in the example just given, what is happening is that before one matter has been thoroughly prayed for the second topic is already being prayed for. Consequently, in a prayer meeting the brethren who are gathered must notice if a prayer burden for the first matter has been discharged. If all pray for that sister and the prayer burden is discharged, the believers can then pray for the sick brother. Before the prayer burden of the first topic has been lifted, those praying together should not switch to the second and third subjects of prayer. Suppose the entire gathering is yet involved with one particular matter. Then no one present should try to inject another prayer that is only according to his own personal feeling.

Brethren should learn to touch the spirit of the entire gathering. They must learn to enter into the feeling of the whole assembly. Let us see that some matters may only need to be prayed once and the burden for such is over and done with. But other matters perhaps need to be prayed twice. While still other matters probably have to be prayed three or five

神前有能 **12**

times before the various burdens for them are discharged. Irrespective of the number of times, the burden must be discharged before prayer on a particular item is ended. The principle of praying three times is none other than to pray until the burden is lifted.

Notes and Meditations from:
Day Twelve – *Prayer and Burden*

13 神前有能

Prayer and Pressure

"IN PRESSURE THOU HAST ENLARGED ME; BE GRACIOUS UNTO ME, AND HEAR MY PRAYER."

Psalm 4.1b Darby

One brother asked me why his prayer went unanswered. My reply was that it was because there was no pressure. When he then asked why pressure was necessary, I told him that for prayer to be answered there must be pressure. As a matter of fact, I often ask brethren this question: does God hear your prayer? The answer I receive is frequently this, that after praying for three or five times the matter is forgotten. Why is it forgotten? Because they do not feel the pressure upon them. Is it not strange that this is often the case?

If you have forgotten a matter for prayer, can you blame God for not remembering it? Naturally God will not answer it for you if you merely utter a few words of prayer casually. Many pray as though they are writing a composition. It would be better for them not to pray at all. The praying of many people violates the very first principle of prayer, which is neither faith nor promise, but need. No need, no prayer. It is no wonder that people do not receive answer to their prayer.

13 神前有能

For God to answer a believer's prayer, He will first give that one a need: He gives the believer some pressure in order for that one to sense a need. And then the believer will turn to God for an answer.

John Knox was powerful in prayer. Queen Mary of England once said, "I am not afraid of the army of all Scotland, I am only fearful of the prayer of John Knox." How did John Knox pray? He said, "O God, give me Scotland or I die!" Why did he pray in such a way? Because the pressure within him was too great. It was beyond his measure, so he poured it out before God. The pressure within John Knox caused him to utter such a prayer.

You may not understand why Moses in his day prayed in such a manner as the following: "Yet now, if thou wilt forgive their sin—; and if not, blot me, I pray thee, out of thy book which thou hast written" (Exodus 32.32). It was because Moses was conscious of a need. He was so pressed by this need that he would rather perish if God did not save the children of Israel. Therefore, God heard him.

Paul's heart was the same; "I could wish that I myself were anathema from Christ for my brethren's sake, my kinsmen according to the flesh" (Romans 9.3). He would rather not be

神前有能

saved if the children of Israel were not saved too. Such a word is not lip service nor is it mere emotional outburst. It comes from a deep feeling caused by the pressure of need. Someone may imitate the words of another's prayer, but that one's prayer will be ineffectual and useless because there is no pressure. Who will pray that if God does not answer him he will not get up? If anyone really has such a feeling and word within him, his prayer will be heard. You too may go and pray with such a word, but the essential thing is that you must sense the pressure within you.

May we thus understand why some prayers are answered and others are not. Why is it that God often hears prayers for big things while He does not hear prayers over small matters? Why is it that God hears our prayers for loved ones, friends or co-workers when they are dangerously ill, but He does not immediately hear our prayers when we have a headache, a cold or have some scratches? I have said before and will say again: any prayer that does not move us cannot move God. It is a matter of power, and power is determined by pressure.

Why does God allow many difficulties, many dead ends and many unavoidable things to come our way? For no other reason than to call us to utilize such pressure and become

13 神前有能

powerful in prayer. Our failure lies in not knowing how to make use of pressure by turning it into power.

We ought to know that all pressures are with purpose. Nevertheless, we are not to wait till the pressure becomes exceedingly unbearable before we pray. We should learn to pray without pressure as well as with pressure. If there is pressure, let us utilize each pressure by converting it into power. By so doing we will come to realize that whenever pressure arises God is going to manifest the power of raising the dead. There is no power greater than resurrection power. And when we are pressed beyond hope, we will experience the power of His resurrection issuing forth from within us.

How many times in your life have your prayers been answered? You no doubt have at least had answers to your prayers a few times. Why were these few prayers answered? Was it not because you sensed pressure, yet because it was too great you poured out your heart before God? Perhaps you had never before fasted, but on that particular day you could not help but fast. You sensed you were being pressed to come before God. You no longer considered prayer all a burden; quite the contrary, prayer for you became that day a means by which to discharge a burden.

神前有能

13

NOTES AND MEDITATIONS FROM:

DAY THIRTEEN – *Prayer and Pressure*

14

神前有能

Pray with the Spirit

"I WILL PRAY WITH THE SPIRIT, AND I WILL PRAY WITH THE
UNDERSTANDING."
1 Corinthians 14.15

Not only should we pray with the spirit; we should
"pray with the mind also" (1 Corinthians 14.15
NAS). In praying, these two must work together. A
believer receives in his spirit what he needs to pray and
understands in his mind what he has received. The spirit
accepts the burden of prayer while the mind formulates that
burden in prayerful words. Only in this way is the prayer of a
believer perfected. How often the Christian prays according
to the thought in his mind without possessing any revelation
in his spirit. He becomes the origin of the prayer himself. But
true prayer must originate from the throne of God. It initially
is sensed in the person's spirit, next is understood by his
mind, and finally is uttered through the power of the Spirit.
Man's spirit and prayer are inseparable.

To be able to pray with the spirit a Christian must learn first
to walk according to the spirit. No one can pray with his
spirit if during the whole day he walks after the flesh. The
state of one's prayer life cannot be too greatly disconnected

from the condition of his daily walk. The spiritual condition of many too often disqualifies them from praying in the spirit. The quality of a man's prayer is determined by the state of his living. How could a fleshly person offer spiritual prayer? A spiritual person, on the other hand, does not necessarily pray spiritually either, for unless he is watchful he also shall fall into the flesh. Nonetheless, should the spiritual man pray often with his spirit, his very praying shall keep his spirit and mind continually in tune with God. Praying exercises the spirit which in turn is strengthened through such exercising. Negligence in prayer withers the inner man. Nothing can be a substitute for it, not even Christian work. Many are so preoccupied with work that they allow little time for prayer. Hence they cannot cast out demons. Prayer enables us first inwardly to overcome the enemy and then outwardly to deal with him. All who have fought against the enemy on their knees shall see him routed upon their rising up.

The burdens of the spirit differ from the weights on the spirit. The latter proceed from Satan with the intent of crushing the believer and making him suffer, but the former issue from God in His desire to manifest His will to the believer so that he may cooperate with Him. Any weight on the spirit has no other objective than to oppress; it therefore usually serves no purpose and produces no fruit. A burden of the

神前有能

spirit, on the other hand, is given by God to His child for the purpose of calling him to work, to pray, or to preach. It is a burden with purpose, with reason, and for spiritual profit. We must learn how to distinguish the burden of the spirit from the weight on the spirit.

Satan never burdens Christians with anything; he only encircles their spirit and presses in with a heavy weight. Such a load binds one's spirit and throttles his mind from functioning. A person with a burden or concern from God merely carries it; but the one who is oppressed by Satan finds his total being bound. With the arrival of the power of darkness, a believer instantaneously forfeits his freedom. A God-given burden is quite the reverse. However weighty it may be, God's concern is never so heavy as to throttle him from praying. The *freedom* of prayer will never be lost under any burden from God: yet the enemy's weight which forces itself upon one's spirit invariably denies one his freedom to pray. The burden imparted by God is lifted once we have prayed, but the heaviness from the enemy cannot be raised unless we fight and resist in prayer. The weight on the spirit steals in unawares, whereas the concern of the spirit results from God's Spirit working in our spirit. The load upon the spirit is most miserable and oppressive, while the burden of the spirit is very joyous (naturally the flesh does not deem it so), for it summons us to walk together with God (see Matthew 11.30). It turns bitter only when opposed and its demand is not met.

All real works begin with burdens or concerns in the spirit. (Of course, when the spirit lacks any concern we need to exercise our minds.) When God desires us to labor or speak or pray, He first implants a burden in our spirit. Now if we are acquainted with the laws of the spirit we will not continue on carelessly with the work in hand and allow the burden to accrue. Nor will we neglectfully disregard the burden until it is no longer sensed. We should lay everything aside immediately to ferret (seek) out the *meaning of this burden*. Once we have discerned its import, we can act accordingly. And when the work called for is done, the burden then leaves us.

In order to receive burdens from God our spirit has to be kept continuously free and untrammeled (open). Only an untrammeled spirit can detect the movement of the Holy Spirit. Any spirit which is already full of concerns has lost the sharpness of its intuitive sense and hence cannot be a good vessel. Due to his failure to act according to the burden which he already has received from God, the believer often finds himself painfully burdened for many days. During this period God is unable to give him any new one.

Consequently, it is highly necessary to search out the meaning of a burden through prayer, with the help of the Holy Spirit and the exercise of one's mind.

Frequently the burden or concern in the spirit is for prayer (Colossians 4.12). As a matter of fact we are not able to pray beyond our burden. To continue to pray without it can produce no fruit because the prayer must be emanating from our mind. But the *prayer* burden in the spirit can only be lightened *through prayer*. Whenever God concerns us with something, such as prayer, preaching the Word, and so forth, the only way to lessen that concern or burden is to do what it calls for. The prayer burden in the spirit alone enables us to pray in the Holy Spirit with sighs too deep for words. When our spirit is concerned with prayer burdens nothing can discharge that burden except prayer. It is lifted soon after the work is performed.

NOTES AND MEDITATIONS FROM:
DAY FOURTEEN – *Pray with the Spirit*

15 神前有能

Pray Thrice

"...OUGHT ALWAYS TO PRAY, AND NOT TO FAINT."
Luke 18.1

"AND HE LEFT THEM AGAIN, AND WENT AWAY, AND PRAYED A
THIRD TIME, SAYING AGAIN THE SAME WORDS."
Matthew 26.44

"CONCERNING THIS THING I BESOUGHT THE LORD THRICE,
THAT IT MIGHT DEPART FROM ME."
2 Corinthians 12.8

There is one particular secret about prayer that we
should know about, which is, a praying three times to
the Lord. This "thrice" is not limited to only three
times, it may be many times. The Lord Jesus asked God three
times in the garden of Gethsemane until His prayer was
heard—at which point He stopped. Paul too prayed to God
three times, and ceased praying after he was given God's
word. Hence all prayers should heed the principle of thrice.
This "thrice" does not mean that we need only pray once,
twice, and three times, and then stop. It simply signifies the
fact that before we stop we must pray thoroughly until God
hears us.

15

神前有能

This principle of three times is most significant. Not only in our personal prayer do we need to pay attention to such a principle, even in our prayer meetings we must attend to it. If we expect our prayer in a prayer meeting to fulfill the ministry of the church in accomplishing whatever God wants us to accomplish, we should well remember this important principle.

The principle of praying thrice is to pray thoroughly, a praying through until we are clear on God's will, until we obtain His answer. In a prayer meeting, never reflect that since a matter has already been prayed for by a certain brother it does not need my prayer anymore. For example, a sister is sick and we pray for her. Not because one brother has already prayed for that sister do I not need to add my prayer. No, that brother has prayed once, I may pray the second time, and another may pray the third time. This does not imply that each prayer must be prayed by three persons. Prayer must be offered with burden. Sometimes we may have to pray five or ten times. What is important is that there needs to be prayer till the burden is discharged. This is the principle of praying thrice. This is the secret to success in a prayer meeting.

Let us not allow our prayer to jump about like a grasshopper: hopping to another matter before the first one is thoroughly prayed through, and before this second matter is thoroughly prayed for, we are found skipping back to the very first matter. Such hopping-around prayer does not discharge burdens, and is therefore difficult to obtain God's answer. Such prayer has little use and does not fulfill the ministry of prayer.

How long ought we to pray such prayer? We know there are many prayers which need to be prayed only once. But prayer which attacks Satan has no fear of being too much. The purpose of this parable which our Lord gives is that we "ought *always* to pray" (Luke 18.1). This judge avenges the widow not for the sake of justice nor for any other reason but because he cannot stand her continual coming. Does he not say to himself, "I will avenge her, lest she wear me out by her continual coming"? Consequently, this kind of prayer should be offered without intermission. Such prayer against the adversary is not merely to be uttered at times of special need, it is to be maintained as an attitude and breathed unceasingly in the spirit in ordinary days when all is calm. The Lord Jesus, in explaining the word of this parable, asks: "And shall not God avenge his elect, that cry to him day and night"? This kind of prayer must therefore be prayed day and night without ceasing. We should accuse our enemy before God incessantly, since we are told in Revelation 12 that

15 神前有能

Satan "accuseth [the brethren] before our God day and night" (v.10). If he accuses us day and night, should we not also accuse him day and night?

This is true vindication: as the devil treats us, so shall we treat him. The cry of this widow continued on until the adversary was judged and punished and she was avenged of her grievance. As long as there is another day in which Satan still usurps the world, and so long as he is not yet imprisoned in the bottomless pit or cast into the lake of fire, we will not cease from praying against him. Not until God has avenged us and Satan has in truth fallen as lightning from heaven shall our prayer come to an end. How much it is the desire of God that we show deeper hatred towards the devil. Have we not suffered enough from him?!? He has shown his enmity towards us at every step of our way, he has caused us to suffer terribly both in body and in spirit; why, then, do we endure his persecution without speech or prayer? Why have we not risen up to accuse him before our God with words of prayer? We ought to seek for vindication. Why do we not continually approach God and accuse the enemy, thus releasing the long-suppressed exasperation? The Lord Jesus is calling us today to oppose the devil with prayer.

15

NOTES AND MEDITATIONS FROM:

DAY FIFTEEN – *Pray Thrice*

16

神前有能

Pray with Tears

"PUT THOU MY TEARS INTO THY BOTTLE; ARE THEY NOT
IN THY BOOK?"

Psalm 56.8b

"Hear my prayer, O Jehovah, and give ear unto my
cry; hold not thy peace at my tears: for I am a
stranger with thee, a sojourner, as all my fathers
were" (Psalm 39.12). Tearful prayer before God is the best
way to be heard. If tears are added to your prayer, it will be
quickly answered. Many prayers are heartless because there
are no tears. If you have heart, why not add your tears? Thus
will you be able, as did the psalmist, to tell God: "I will not
be long on this earth, for I am only a stranger and sojourner.
It is miserable enough for me to be in this world, so please
hear me." And God will surely hear our prayers. Though
there is no merit in the tears themselves, yet they do express
what is in your heart; that is to say, you really have a heart
desire. May we therefore add more tears to our prayers that
we may be heard.

"Turn back, and say to Hezekiah the prince of my people,
Thus saith Jehovah, the God of David thy father, I have
heard thy prayer, I have seen thy tears: behold, I will heal

16 神前有能

thee; on the third day thou shalt go up unto the house of Jehovah" (2 Kings 20.5). How good a word this is! God sees our tears! Hezekiah prayed to God for more days to live, and he also wept. And God answered him. This shows how the Lord is pleased with our tearful prayers; such prayers can move His heart. In view of this, then whatever matter which cannot move *your* heart to tears cannot move *God's* heart either. Hence it behooves us to shed more tears before the Lord. A weeping before men reveals your weakness, in that you lack the mien (dignity) of a man; but a not weeping before God manifests that you are as numb as wood and stone.

I personally treasure very much this word in 2 Kings 20.5: "I have seen thy tears." Each time we meet a difficult situation which is heartbreaking, distressing, pressed beyond measure and with no way out, we can lift up our heads and drop a few tears before God, for He surely sees. Yet be clear of this, that tears are futile if they are not shed before God. Naturally, there are many people in this world who are prone to weeping. Man's cry simply expresses his own sorrow and distress; it in itself will not produce any positive result. Tears with prayer, however, are effective. Every time you cry in distress, why not add to it prayer? You may tell God your sorrow and distress through prayer. The Bible shows us not only the tearful prayer of Hezekiah but also

神前有能

the prayers and supplications of our Lord which came with strong crying and tears (see Hebrews 5.7).

Oftentimes it is useless to cry to each other; but if one cries to God it is effective, since God sees one's tears and will hear one's prayer. Indeed, every drop of tears shed before God will be counted by Him—"Thou numberest my wanderings: put thou my tears into thy bottle; are they not in thy book?" (Psalm 56.8) Please note that such is the advantage of having tears before God. O sorrowful heart, if life makes you suffer, and you are pressed beyond measure, passing your days in misery, and weary in battling many problems, why not cry before God? Let me tell you, this will never fail. God will record the tears you shed each time. He will put them in His bottle, which means He will remember all your sufferings. Thank God, our tears do not fall to the ground and mix with the dust; rather, they are stored in God's bottle of remembrance; for are they not in His record-books? God will not forget; He will always remember our tears.

Let me ask you a question. Do you know what kind of cry is most comforting and satisfying? When does a child cry the loudest and strongest? It is not at the time when he is beaten nor when he is hungry, but at the first instance that he sees his dear mother at home after he has been insulted and

16

troubled by people on the outside. At that moment he will cry very loud and very long. Oh, to cry before a lover is most consoling. There is neither meaning nor effect to cry before ordinary people. Where and when should we therefore cry? Undoubtedly before the God who cares most for us and who is the dearest to us. Let us cry our heart out before Him, for He treasures us. It is most comforting to cry before the Lord because He is listening and seeing. He will perform that which we ask for. Oh, we surely will reap the best consequence if we weep before God.

Let us further consider the advantage of tearful prayer as we look into the story recorded in Mark 9 of the father and the son. "Straightway the father of the child cried out, and said, I believe; help thou mine unbelief" (v.24). At that moment the father's heart was suffering greatly, and he hated himself for his unbelief. The father had witnessed the intense suffering of his child and had tried everything without result. And then he had asked the disciples of the Lord to help, but that too had been of no avail. He was therefore really desperate now. Under such anguish and anxiety, he could not help but cry out immediately to the Lord. And what was the outcome? The outcome was that the Lord heard his prayer, and the child was healed. We need to see that many prayers are ineffectual for the simple reason that there are no tears.

16

"How unceasing is my remembrance of thee in my supplications, night and day longing to see thee, remembering thy tears, that I may be filled with joy" (2 Timothy 1.3-4). Why did Paul long to see Timothy? Because of the tears of Timothy. In the Bible those who serve the Lord seem all to be persons who know how to weep. So that I believe that no one who serves the Lord well will be exempt from shedding tears. Tears appear to be a necessity to workers. It is therefore best if tears are mingled with prayer for God to remember and to hear.

NOTES AND MEDITATIONS FROM:
DAY SIXTEEN – *Pray with Tears*

17

神前有能

Watch and Pray

"WITH ALL PRAYER AND SUPPLICATION PRAYING AT ALL SEASONS
IN THE SPIRIT, AND WATCHING THEREUNTO IN ALL PERSEVERANCE
AND SUPPLICATION FOR ALL THE SAINTS."

Ephesians 6.18

The fragment of this verse upon which our attention
will be focused is "watching thereunto in all perseverance". What does the word "thereunto" point towards?
By reading the preceding clause we realize that it points at
prayer and supplication. What the apostle means to say is
that "with all prayer and supplication praying at all seasons
in the Spirit" is still not enough, but that "watching . . . in all
perseverance" must be added to prayer and supplication. In
other words, there needs to be prayer on the one side and a
watching on the other. What does "watching" mean? It
means not slumbering; it means supervising or looking with
eyes open; it means preventing any danger or emergency.
Watching in prayer and supplication bespeaks (speaks of)
having spiritual insight to discern the wiles of Satan and to
discover the latter's end and means. Let us now enter concretely into some of the aspects of watching in supplication
and prayer.

17　　神前有能

Prayer is a kind of service. It ought to be placed in a preeminent position. Satan always maneuvers to put other things concerning the Lord before prayer and to place prayer at the very last. However much people are reminded of the importance of prayer, not many really appreciate it. People are usually enthusiastic in attending meetings for ministry, Bible study, and so forth. They will find time for such meetings. But when it comes to prayer meeting, the attendance is so surprisingly minimal. No matter how many messages are given to remind us that our principal service is prayer and that if we fail in our prayer life we fail in everything, prayer is still not esteemed and is treated as a matter of little consequence. Faced with a pile of problems, we may say with our lips that only prayer can solve them, yet we talk more than pray, worry more than pray, and scheme more than pray. In sum, everything is put before prayer; other things are placed in prominent positions while prayer is relegated to last place; it is the only thing which is not so important.

One who knows the Lord deeply once said, "We all have committed the sin of neglecting prayer; we should tell ourselves: You are that man." We should say to ourselves indeed: You are the man! We should not blame others for not praying; we ourselves need to repent. How we need the Lord to enlighten our eyes that we may comprehend afresh the importance of prayer and know anew its value. Furthermore, we must recognize that had Satan not deceived us, we would not be neglecting prayer so much. We should therefore watch and discover all the various wiles of Satan. We will not allow him to delude us any more in relaxing in prayer.

Brethren, we must fight for the prayer time, we must have time to pray. If we wait until we have some leisure moments to pray, we will never have the chance to pray. We should set apart some definite time for prayer. "Those who have no set time for prayer," warns Andrew Murray, "do not pray." For this reason, we need to watch that we may get time to pray. We must also use prayer to protect this prayer time from being snatched away through the wiles of the devil.

We must not only be watchful in keeping the time of prayer but also be watchful during the prayer time so that we may really pray. For Satan will use his tricks to hinder our prayer while we are actually on our knees, just as he has previously made use of outward situations and all sorts of things to oppress us and thus keep us from having any time to pray in the first place.

Our mind is clear and our thought is concentrated; but as soon as we kneel down to pray our thoughts commence to be scattered: what should not be recalled is recalled, what should not be premeditated is premeditated, and many unnecessary notions suddenly dart in. All these thoughts were absent before prayer; but they now crowd in to disturb us just at the time of prayer.

A battle is involved here. Before we pray we should first use prayer to ask God to enable us to pray; and during the time of prayer we should ask God to help us pray single-mindedly that our prayer will not be obstructed by any device of the enemy. We will speak to those disturbing thoughts, voices, weaknesses, and sicknesses: I oppose all these causeless phenomena as lies, as Satanic counterfeits. We will utter our voice to drive them away, we will not give any ground to the enemy. We must watch and resist the wiles of Satan with prayer that we may not only pray but pray through as well.

To pray through and to pray with strength is not a vain expectation. Ease and comfort will not get us into this prayer life, neither will we ever drift into this prayer life. We must learn a little, break a little, and fight a little to obtain such prayer.

17

NOTES AND MEDITATIONS FROM:

DAY SEVENTEEN – *Watch and Pray*

18

神前有能

Do Not Pray Amiss

"YE ASK, AND RECEIVE NOT, BECAUSE YE ASK AMISS, THAT YE MAY
SPEND IT IN YOUR PLEASURES."
James 4.3

Men ought to ask of God. Scripture, however, lays down a second condition: do not ask amiss. "Ye ask, and receive not, because ye ask amiss" (James 4.3). Men may ask God for their needs, but they are not supposed to ask unreasonably or beyond their measure. It requires a few years of learning before anyone can pray so-called "big prayers" before God.

In the early days of our spiritual life, it is rather difficult for us to differentiate between big prayers and praying amiss. It is best for us at the beginning not to ask according to our lusts nor to ask wantonly (carelessly) for what we are not in need of. God will only supply our need and give us that which is necessary. Many times, though, God does grant us exceedingly abundantly above all that we ask. But if the young ask wrongly they will not be heard.

What is meant by asking amiss? It means asking beyond your measure, beyond your need, beyond your actual want.

18

神前有能

For instance, I have a certain need and I ask God to supply it. I ask according to the amount of my need. If I ask beyond my need, I will be asking amiss. If my need is great, I can ask God to supply that great need. But I should not ask for more, for God has no delight in hearing flippant prayer. Prayer ought to be measured by need; it should not be offered recklessly.

To ask amiss is like a four-year old child asking for the moon in heaven. It is far beyond his need. Likewise, young believers should learn to keep their place in prayer. Only after they have more spiritual experience should they pray big prayers. But for now, let them pray within measure. Let them not open their mouths too wide lest they exceed the limit of actual need.

It may be that men have asked and have not asked wrongly, yet still are not heard. Why? Perhaps it is because there is a basic hindrance—sin standing between God and man.

"If I regard iniquity in my heart, The Lord will not hear" (Psalm 66.18). If anyone has a known sin in his heart and his heart clings to it, he shall not be heard. What is meant by regarding iniquity in the heart? It simply means there is a sin which one in his heart will not give up. Though a person may have great weaknesses, God will forgive them. But if one has a sin of which he is aware and yet still desires it in his heart, then it is more than a weakness in outward conduct; it is regarding iniquity in his heart.

The man in Romans 7 is quite different. He declares that what he does is something which he hates. He has failed, but he hates that failure. The man, however, who regards iniquity in his heart is one who will not give up his sin. He neither gives it up in his conduct nor in his heart. The Lord will not hear the prayer of such a person, for sin has hindered his prayer from being answered.

Special attention should be paid by new believers to reject all known sins. We must learn to live a holy life before God. If anyone is lax in the matter of sin, his prayer will definitely be hindered. Sin is a big problem. Many cannot pray because they tolerate sin in their lives. Sin will not only obstruct our prayers, it will also wreck our conscience.

The effects of sin are two-sided: objectively, there is an effect Godward; subjectively, there is an effect usward.

Objectively, sin obstructs God's grace and God's answer. "Behold, Jehovah's hand is not shortened, that it cannot

18　　　　　　神前有能

save; neither his ear heavy, that it cannot hear: but your iniq-uities have separated between you and your God, and your sins have hid his face from you, so that he will not hear" (Isaiah 59.1-2). God's mercy and grace is the greatest force in the world. Nothing can stand against it except sin. It is said in the Psalms, "If I regard iniquity in my heart, the Lord will not hear" (Psalm 66.18). If a person neglects dealing with sin, there will be an obstruction between him and God. Any unconfessed sin, any sin which is not put under the blood, becomes a great hindrance before God—it hinders prayer from being answered. This is the objective effect of sin.

Subjectively, sin damages a man's conscience. Whenever a person sins, his conscience becomes weakened and depressed irrespective of how hard he tries to convince him-self, of how much he reads the Bible, and of how desperately he holds on to the promises in the Bible and the acceptable grace of God. His conscience is like a ship (see 1 Timothy 1.19). It is all right for a ship to be old, but it cannot be wrecked. It is all right for a ship to be small, but it cannot afford to be broken. In like manner, a conscience must not be wrecked. If the conscience lacks peace, there will be a hindrance in the person and before God.

I often think of the relationship between faith and

18

conscience. Faith is like the cargo and conscience is like the ship. The cargo is in the ship. If the ship is wrecked, the cargo will fall out. When conscience is strong, faith is also strong; but when conscience is wrecked, faith leaks out. God's heart is greater than ours; if we condemn ourselves, how much more will God condemn us. This is what the apostle John tells us (1 John 3.20).

NOTES AND MEDITATIONS FROM:

DAY EIGHTEEN – *Do Not Pray Amiss*

19

神前有能

Do Not Give Up

"REJOICE ALWAYS; PRAY WITHOUT CEASING; IN EVERYTHING GIVE
THANKS; FOR THIS IS THE WILL OF GOD."
1 Thessalonians 5.16-18

To new believers, permit me to say something out of
my experience. Prayer may be divided into two parts:
the first part is praying without any promise until the
promise is given, praying without God's word to having
God's word. All prayers begin this way. Pray by asking God,
and keep on asking. In George Muller's case, some prayers
were answered in one minute while some were not yet
heard even after seven years. This part is the praying part.
The second part is praying from the point at which the
promise is given to the realization of the promise, from having God's word to the fulfillment of His word. During this
period, there should be praise, not prayer. So, the first part is
prayer and the second part is praise. Pray in the first part
from no word to God's word. Praise in the second part from
having the promise till the promise is fulfilled. This is the
secret of prayer.

To the people of this world, prayer has only two focal points: I
have not, so I pray; after I pray, God gives to me. For example:

19　　　神前有能

I prayed yesterday for a watch. After several days, the Lord does give me a watch. This is from nothing to something. But to Christians, there is a third point, a point in between these two: faith. If I pray for a watch and one day am able to claim that God has heard my prayer, then I have reached the point of faith, I know inwardly that I have the watch though my two hands are still empty. A few days later, the watch arrives. Christians need to know how to receive in the spirit; otherwise they have neither faith nor spiritual insight.

Men ought to pray earnestly; they should pray till faith is given. We may say that the first part is praying from no faith to faith; the second part is praising from faith to actual possession. Why should we divide prayer into these two parts? Because once having faith, one can only praise, not pray. If he continues to pray, his faith will be lost. He should use praise to remind God, to speed up the fulfillment. God has already promised to give, what more can he ask? Brothers and sisters all over the world have had such experiences— after faith is given, further prayer is impossible. The one thing to do is to say, "I praise you, Lord." Alas, some brothers do not have this knowledge. God has already promised, yet they keep on praying; and so they pray till they lose everything. This, indeed, is a great loss.

19

How should one maintain one's faith? By praising the Lord: "O Lord, I praise You, for You have heard my prayer. You heard me a month ago." How precious are the words in Mark 11.24. Nowhere in the New Testament is faith more expressed than in that precious verse. "All things whatsoever ye pray and ask for, believe that ye receive them, and ye shall have them." There are three main points here: (a) pray, with nothing in hand, (b) believe, still with nothing, and (c) believe, and the thing is in hand. May new believers really understand what prayer is and know how great a part prayer plays in their lives.

There is another side of prayer which may seem contradictory to what we have just said but which is equally real; it is, men "ought always to pray, and not to faint" (Luke 18.1). The Lord shows us that some prayers require persistency. We must keep on praying till the Lord is worn out, as it were, by our continual coming. This is not a sign of unbelief, rather it is just another kind of faith, "Nevertheless, when the Son of man cometh, shall he find faith on the earth?" says the Lord. This is the kind of faith which believes that by praying persistently God will eventually answer, with or without a previous promise.

Oftentimes we neither do nor can we pray the second time

for we have not actually asked for anything. How many of our prayers have we prayed two, three, five or ten times? Many prayers once we offer them are forgotten. Need we wonder that God also forgets them? We can pray and keep on praying only when there is a real need. Then we are under a sort of environment which presses us and moves us to pray. After fifty years have gone by, we may still remember that prayer. O Lord, if you do not act, I will keep on praying.

Such prayer does not conflict with that in Mark 11. Mark tells us that we ought to pray till we are given faith; here in Luke it tells us that we ought to pray always and not to faint. Many of our prayers are so without heart that they are soon forgotten by the offerers. How can we expect God to hear such heartless prayers? We ourselves have forgotten and yet we wish God would remember. There is no such thing. Therefore, young brothers and sisters should learn how to pray and how to pray till they have received what they have asked for.

A certain sister prayed many years for her brother. God did not seem to hear and the situation grew worse. However, one day she declared that she knew her brother would be saved. She looked as if she had great assurance. From where did she get this assurance? It was because she had read the story of the widow pleading with an unjust judge to avenge her of her adversary. She said, "God has shown me that I have never troubled Him enough. Early in the morning I will ask God to save my brother, at noon I will ask again for the salvation of my brother, and in the evening I will remind Him again of the same. If I pray day and night, from dawn to dusk, then one day God will be so worn out by me that He will say, 'All right, I will grant salvation to your brother!' I have determined to pray in this way. Therefore I know my brother will be saved." This sister had really mastered Luke 18.5.

Naturally speaking this sister was a timid person, but now she became exceedingly bold. She troubled God to the extent that God could do nothing but save her brother. After a week her brother was saved! The light she received from the Bible was terrific. What nature could not make of her, light from heaven did; she was transformed into a "violent" person.

Therefore, if you are asking for something, you must learn to trouble God. How can you expect Him to hear you if you yourself have forgotten what you have asked for? If your need is real, you will pray always and faint not. Pray till God has to hear you.

19

神前有能

Notes and Meditations from:

Day Nineteen – *Do Not Give Up*

神前有能

PART THREE

Powerful According To God

神前有能

The Three Aspects of Prayer

"WITH ALL PRAYER AND SUPPLICATION PRAYING AT ALL SEASONS IN THE SPIRIT, AND WATCHING THEREUNTO IN ALL PERSEVERANCE AND SUPPLICATION FOR ALL THE SAINTS."

Ephesians 6.18

Our prayer has these three aspects: (1) we ourselves, (2) the God to whom we pray, and (3) our enemy, Satan. Every true prayer is related to all three aspects. When we come to pray, we naturally pray for our own welfare. We have needs, wants and expectations; and so we pray. We pray for the sake of fulfilling our requests. Even so, in true prayer we should not simply ask concerning those things pertaining to our own welfare, we should also pray for the glory of God and for heaven's rule over the earth. Although in having prayer answered we who pray are benefited as the immediate beneficiaries, the reality in the spiritual realm shows likewise that the Lord gets glory and that His will is done. Answer to prayer gives the Lord much glory, for it reveals the exceeding greatness of His love and power in fulfilling the request of His children. It also indicates that His will is done, because He will not answer prayer which is not in accordance with His will.

神前有能

The petitioners are we; the petitioned is God. In a successful prayer, both the petitioner and the petitioned gain. The petitioner obtains his heart desire, and the petitioned gets His will done. This we do not need to dwell on at any length, since all of the Lord's faithful children who have some experience in prayer know the relation between those two aspects in prayer. But what we would like to remind believers of now is the fact that if in prayer we only attend to these two aspects of God and man, our prayer is yet imperfect. Even though it may be quite effective, there nevertheless is defeat in success for we still have not mastered the true meaning of prayer. No doubt all spiritual believers are aware of the absolute relationship between prayer and God's glory and will. Prayer is not just for our own profit. Still, such knowledge is incomplete. We must also notice the third aspect: that as we pray to the Lord, what we ask and what God promises will unquestionably hurt His enemy.

We know the ruler of this universe is God. Yet Satan is called "the prince of the world" (John 14.30) since "the whole world lieth in the evil one" (1 John 5.19). Hence we see that there are two diametrically opposing forces in this world, each seeking for ascendancy. God in truth has the ultimate victory; nonetheless, in this age of ours before the millennial kingdom, Satan continues to usurp power in this world to

神前有能

20

oppose God's work, will, and interest. We who are children of God belong to God. If we gain anything under His hand, it naturally will mean that His enemy suffers loss. The amount of gain we make is the amount of God's will done. And the amount of God's will done is in turn the amount of loss Satan suffers.

Since we belong to God, Satan intends to frustrate, afflict, or suppress us and allow us no foothold. This is his aim, although his aim may not be achieved because we may approach the throne of grace by the precious blood of the Lord Jesus, asking for God's protection and care. As God hears our prayer, Satan's plan is definitely defeated. In answering our prayer God thwarts the evil will of Satan, and consequently the latter is not able to ill-treat us according to this scheme. Whatever we gain in prayer is the enemy's loss. So that our gain and the Lord's glory are in inverse proportion to Satan's loss. One gains, the other loses; one loses and the other gains. In view of this, we in our prayer should not only consider our own welfare and the glory and will of God but also observe the third aspect—that which pertains to the enemy, Satan. A prayer that does not take into consideration all three aspects is superficial, of little worth, and without much accomplishment.

神前有能

Nevertheless, very few Christians consider the third aspect—that of Satan—in their prayer. The aim of a true prayer touches on not just personal gain (sometimes this aspect is not even thought of) but more importantly on the glory of God and the loss of the enemy. They do not reckon their own welfare to be of prime importance. They instead consider their prayer to be highly successful if it will cause Satan to lose and God to be glorified. What they look for in their prayer is the enemy's loss. Their view is not restricted to their immediate environment but they take as their perspective God's work and will in the whole world. Yet let me add that this is not to suggest that they only take into account the aspects of God and Satan and entirely forget the personal aspect of prayer. As a matter of fact, when God's will is done and Satan suffers loss they will unquestionably be profited themselves. The spiritual progress of a saint can therefore be judged by the emphasis to be seen in his prayer.

In the parable recorded in Luke 18.1-8 our Lord Jesus touches upon all three features in prayer of which we have been speaking. In this connection, please note that we find three persons mentioned in the parable, namely: (1) the judge, (2) the widow, and (3) the adversary. The judge (in a negative way) represents God, the widow is representative of the church today or individual faithful Christians, while the

神前有能 **20**

adversary stands for our enemy the devil. When we explain this parable we frequently pay attention only to the relation between the judge and the widow. We note how this judge, who neither fears God nor regards men, finally avenges the widow because of her incessant coming; and, we conclude, since our God is not at all virtueless as is this judge, will He not surely avenge us speedily if we pray? Now this is about all that we explain from this parable.

Yet too many of us are unaware of the fact that we are neglecting another important person in the parable. Let us see that if there is no adversary, would this widow find it necessary to go to the judge? Yet she is driven to seek out the judge because she is oppressed by the adversary. Especially when we consider the words which this widow says to the judge, we cannot fail to recognize the place the adversary has in the story. For the sake of brevity the Scripture merely records these few words: "Avenge me of mine adversary"—yet how very much is contained in such a short sentence! Does it not tell of a most agonizing situation? Asking for vengeance reveals that there are wrongs. Where do such wrongs and grievances come from? None other than from the oppression of the defendant—the adversary: and thus is uncovered the deep enmity which exists between him and the widow. It also tells of the severe harassment this widow has suffered at the hands of the adversary. What she complains of before the judge must undoubtedly be a rehearsal of her past experiences and of her current situation. What she asks for is that the judge may avenge her the wrongs done to her by bringing the adversary to justice.

In one sense this adversary is the central figure of the parable. Without him there would be no disturbance created under the judicial rule of the judge; nor, of course, would the widow be troubled—she could quite easily live in peace. Unquestionably, without the adversary there would be no story nor parable, for the one who stirs up all the troubles is this adversary: he is the instigator of all confusions and afflictions.

神前有能

20

NOTES AND MEDITATIONS FROM:

DAY TWENTY – *The Three Aspects of Prayer*

神前有能

Prayer – The Ministry of the Church

"MY HOUSE SHALL BE CALLED A HOUSE OF PRAYER
FOR ALL PEOPLES."
Isaiah 56.77

The prayer ministry of the church is a praying on earth so as to cause action in heaven. We should remember that prayer such as is given in Matthew 18 is definitely not included in devotional prayer or in private personal prayer. Many times we have personal needs for which we ask God and He answers us. There is indeed a place for personal prayer. Likewise, oftentimes we sense the nearness of God. Thank God, He hears devotional prayers. This too should not be despised. We even acknowledge that should the prayer of a brother or sister go unanswered or should a person not sense the nearness of God, something is wrong. We should pay attention to personal prayer as well as devotional prayer. Especially with young believers, they shall not be able to run the course before them if they are lacking in personal and devotional prayers.

Even so, we need to realize that prayer is not just for personal use, nor is it only for devotional purpose. Prayer is a ministry, prayer is a work. This prayer on earth is the church's ministry as well as her work. It is the responsibility of the church before God, because her prayer is the outlet of heaven. What is the prayer of the church? God desires to do a certain thing, and the church on earth prays for this thing in anticipation so that it may be realized on earth and that God's purpose may be accomplished.

The ministry of the church is the ministry of the body of Christ, and that ministry is prayer. Such prayer is neither for devotional purpose nor for personal need; it is more for "heaven". Now what such prayer as this—in the instance before us here—signifies is as follows (see Matthew 18.15-20): Here is a man who has lost fellowship due to his refusal to listen to the persuasion of one brother, to the advice of two or three other brothers, and finally to the judgment of the church. God will therefore loose a judgment upon him as to be considered a Gentile and a publican; yet God will not act immediately but will wait until the church prays towards that end, and then He will do it in heaven. If the church will take up the responsibility to pray on earth such as this, it will eventually be noticed that this offending man's spiritual life shall begin to dry up as though he has no part with God thereafter. God will undertake to do this, but He awaits the church to pray.

神前有能

21

Many matters are piled up in heaven, many transactions remain undone, simply because God is unable to find His outlet on earth. Who knows how very many unfinished matters there are in heaven which God cannot execute because the church has not exercised her free will to stand on His side for the realization of His purpose. Let us understand that the church's noblest work, the greatest task she could ever undertake, is to be the outlet for God's will. For the church to be the outlet of God's will is for her to pray. Such prayer is not fragmentary; it is a prayer ministry—prayer as work. As God gives vision and opens people's eyes to see His will, so people rise up to pray.

The Lord shows us here that individual prayer is inadequate; it takes at least two to pray. If we do not see this, we will not be able to know what the Lord is talking about. The prayers in the Gospel according to John are all personal. Hence we find such a word as: "Whatsoever ye shall ask of the Father in my name, he may give it you" (15.16). There is no condition laid down as to the number of persons. In Matthew 18, however, a numerical condition is given; namely, at least two. "If two of you . . . on earth . . .", says the Lord. There needs to be at least two because in this passage we have the matter of fellowship. It is not something done by one person, nor is it one person who serves as God's outlet, but it is two.

21　　　　神前有能

The principle of two persons is the principle of the church, which is also the principle of the body of Christ. Though such prayer is prayed by two persons, to "agree" is indispensable. To agree is to be harmonious. Those two individuals must be harmonious, must stand on the ground of the body, and must know what the life of the body is. These two here have but one aim, which is to say to God: We want Your will to be done—as in heaven, so on earth. When the church stands on such a ground and prays accordingly, we will see that whatever is prayed shall be done by the heavenly Father.

When we truly stand on the ground of the church and take up this responsibility of prayer ministry before God, the will of God shall be done in the church where we are. Otherwise, the church in one's locality is vain. Such prayer, whether prayed by few or by many, must be a strong prayer. For the degree of God's working today is governed by the degree of the prayer of the church. The manifestation of God's power may not exceed the prayer of the church. Today the greatness of God's power is circumscribed by the greatness of the church's prayer. This does not mean, of course, that the power of God in heaven is only that great and no more, for obviously in heaven His power is unlimited. Only on earth today is the manifestation of His power dependent on how much the church prays. Only by the prayer of the church can

神前有能 21

the manifested power of God be measured.

In view of this, the church should pray big prayers and make big requests. How can the church pray small prayers when she comes before the God of such abundance? She cannot make little requests before such a great God. To come before the great God is to expect great things to happen. If the capacity of the church is limited, it cannot help but restrict the manifestation of God's power. Let it be recognized that the matter of the overcomers has not yet been fully solved nor has Satan been cast into the bottomless pit. For the sake of His testimony, therefore, God must obtain a vessel through which He may do all His works. It needs the church to pray tremendous prayers in order to manifest God. And this is the ministry of the church.

Brothers and sisters, we wonder whether God, in visiting our prayer meeting, can confirm that it truly fulfills the prayer ministry of the church. We must see that it is not a question of the number of times, rather is it a matter of whether there is weight. If we really see the prayer responsibility of the church, we cannot but confess how inadequate is our prayer, how we have restricted God and hindered Him from doing all He wants to do. The church has failed in her ministry! How mournful is this situation!

21 神前有能

Whether or not God is able to have a church which is faithful to her ministry depends on whether a group of people disqualify themselves before God or become true vessels of His in the realization of His purpose. We want to shout forth that what God looks for is the faithfulness of the church to her ministry. The ministry of the church is prayer—not the ordinary kind consisting of small prayers but the kind which prepares the way of God. It is God who first desires to do a certain thing, but the church prepares the way for it with prayer so that He may have a thoroughfare. The church should have big prayers, terrific and strong prayers. Prayer is not a light matter before God. If prayer is always centered upon self, upon personal problems and upon small gain or loss, where can there be the way for the eternal purpose of God to get through? We need to be pushed to the depth in this matter of prayer.

NOTES AND MEDITATIONS FROM:

DAY TWENTY ONE – *Prayer - The Ministry of the Church*

神前有能

Earth Governs Heaven

"VERILY I SAY UNTO YOU, WHAT THINGS SOEVER YE SHALL BIND ON
EARTH SHALL BE BOUND IN HEAVEN; AND WHAT THINGS SOEVER YE
SHALL LOOSE ON EARTH SHALL BE LOOSED IN HEAVEN."
Matthew 18.18

"Verily I say unto you, What things soever ye shall
bind on earth shall be bound in heaven; and what
things soever ye shall loose on earth shall be
loosed in heaven." What is characteristic of this verse? The
peculiar point here is that the action on earth precedes the
action in heaven. Not that heaven binds first, but that the
earth binds first; not that heaven looses first, but that the
earth looses first. Since the earth has already bound it, heav-
en will also bind it; since the earth has loosed it, heaven will
also loose it. The action of heaven is governed by the action
on earth. All that contradicts God needs to be bound, and all
that agrees with God needs to be loosed. Whatever the thing
may be, whether it should be bound or loosed, such action
of binding and loosing begins on earth. The action on earth
precedes the action in heaven, for the earth governs heaven.

Let us use some Old Testament examples to illustrate how

神前有能

the earth governs heaven. When Moses on top of the hill held up his hand, Israel prevailed; but when he let down his hand, Amalek prevailed (see Exodus 17.9-11). Who decided the victory or defeat at the foot of the hill? Was it God who willed it or was it Moses? Here we see the principle of God's working, the secret of His action: whatever He wills to do, if man does not will it, He will not do it. We cannot make God do what He does not want to do, but we can hinder Him from doing what He does wish to do. In heaven the issue is decided by God, but before men it is decided by Moses. In heaven God wants the children of Israel to win; yet on earth, if Moses does not hold up his hand Israel will be defeated, but if indeed he holds up his hand Israel will win. The earth governs heaven.

"Thus saith the Lord Jehovah: For this, moreover, will I be inquired of by the house of Israel, to do it for them: I will increase them with men like a flock" (Ezekiel 36.37). God has a purpose, which is, to increase the number of the house of Israel like a flock. Those who do not know God will say that if He wants to increase the house of Israel like a flock why does He not simply give the increase, for who can stand against Him? But here is the word which God declares—that if He be inquired of concerning this matter by the house of Israel He will do it for them. The principle is unmistakable:

神前有能 22

God has a purpose already determined, but He will not forthwith (immediately) do it until He is inquired of by the house of Israel. He wants the earth to govern heaven.

"Thus saith Jehovah, the Holy One of Israel, and his Maker: Ask me of the things that are to come; concerning my sons, and concerning the work of my hands, command ye me" (Isaiah 45.11). This is a most amazing statement. Are we surprised? Concerning His sons and His work, God says "Command ye me." People dare not utter these three words—"Command ye me"—for how can man ever command God? All who know Him realize that no presumptuous word should ever be uttered before God. Yet He Himself offers this word to us: "Concerning my sons and concerning the work of my hands, command ye me." This is none other than earth governing heaven.

Now obviously this in no way can imply that we can force God to do what He will *not* do; not at all. Rather, it simply means that we may command Him to do what He *desires* to do. And this shall be the ground on which we stand. It is because we know God's will that we may say to Him: "God, we want You to do this thing, we are determined that You do it, You cannot but do it." And thus shall we have strong and powerful prayer. How we need to ask God to open our eyes

神前有能

that we may see how His work is done in this dispensation. For during this present age all the works of God are done on this very ground: Heaven desires to do, but heaven will not act right away; it waits for the earth to do first, and then it will do it. Though earth stands second, it nevertheless is also first. Heaven will move only after earth has moved. For God wills to have the earth govern heaven.

"What things soever ye shall bind on earth shall be bound in heaven; and what things soever ye shall loose on earth shall be loosed in heaven" (v.18). Who are the "ye" here? They are the church, because in the preceding verse the Lord mentions the church. So that this is a continuation of verse 17. Therefore, the meaning of this verse 18 now before us is: that whatever things you the church shall bind on earth shall be bound in heaven, and whatever things you the church shall loose on earth shall be loosed in heaven.

Here lies a most important principle: God works through the church today; He cannot do whatever He desires to do unless He does it through the church. This is a most sobering principle. Today God cannot do things by His own Self alone, because there is in existence another free will; without the cooperation of that will God is not able to do anything. The measure of the power of the church today determines

神前有能

the measure of the manifestation of the power of God. For His power is now revealed through the church. God has put Himself in the church. If she is able to arrive at a high and great position, the manifestation of the power of God can also arrive at such a high and great position. If the church is unable to reach a high and great position, then God too cannot manifest His power in highness and greatness.

This whole matter can be likened to the flow of water in one's house. Though the water tank of the Water Supply Company is huge, its flow is limited to the diameter of the water pipe in one's house. If a person wishes to have more flow of water, he will need to enlarge his water pipe. Today the degree of the manifestation of God's power is governed by the capacity of the church. Just as at one time earlier, when God manifested Himself in Christ, His manifestation was as large as the capacity of Christ; so now, God's manifestation in the church is likewise circumscribed—this time by the capacity of the church. The greater the capacity of the church, the greater the manifestation of God, and the fuller the knowledge of God.

We need to see that in all the things which God does on earth today He will first get the church to stand with Him, and then He will do the work through her. God will not execute anything independently; whatever He does today He does with the cooperation of the church. She is that through which God manifests Himself.

Let us repeat that the church is like a water pipe. If the pipe is small it will not be able to convey much water even should the source be as watery as the Yangtze River. God in heaven purposes to do something, but He will not perform it until there is movement on earth. How many are the things which God wants to bind and to loose in heaven! Many are the people and things that are contradictory to Him; and all these God expects to be bound. Many also are those people and things that are spiritual, valuable, profitable, sanctified, and being of God; and these He anticipates to be loosed. But just here a problem arises: Will there be man on earth who will first bind what God wants to bind and loose what He intends to loose? God wills to have the earth govern heaven; He desires His church on earth to govern heaven.

This does not imply that God is not all-mighty, for He is indeed the Almighty God. Yet the all-mightiness of God can only be manifested on earth through a channel. We cannot increase God's power, but we can hinder it. Man is not able to give increase to God's power, nonetheless he can obstruct it. We cannot ask God to do what He does not want to do,

22

yet we can restrict Him from doing that which He does want
to do. Do we really see this? The church has a power by
which to manage the power of God. She can either permit
God to do what He wants or else prohibit Him from doing it.

Our eyes need to foreglimpse the future. One day God will
extend His church to be the New Jerusalem, and at that time
His glory will be fully manifested through the church without encountering any difficulty. Today God wants the church
to loose on earth first before He will loose in heaven; He
wants her to bind on earth first before He will bind in heav-
en. Heaven will not begin to do things. Heaven will only follow earth in its working. God will not start first; He in His
operation only follows the church. Oh, if this be the case,
what a tremendous responsibility the church has!

NOTES AND MEDITATIONS FROM:
DAY TWENTY TWO – *Earth Governs Heaven*

23

神前有能

Harmony in the Holy Spirit

"THESE ALL WITH ONE ACCORD CONTINUED STEADFASTLY
IN PRAYER."
Acts 1.14a

"VERILY I SAY UNTO YOU, WHAT THINGS SOEVER YE SHALL BIND ON
EARTH SHALL BE BOUND IN HEAVEN; AND WHAT THINGS SOEVER YE
SHALL LOOSE ON EARTH SHALL BE LOOSED IN HEAVEN. AGAIN I
SAY UNTO YOU, THAT IF TWO OF YOU SHALL AGREE ON EARTH AS
TOUCHING ANYTHING THAT THEY SHALL ASK, IT SHALL BE DONE
FOR THEM BY MY FATHER WHO IS IN HEAVEN. FOR WHERE TWO OR
THREE ARE GATHERED TOGETHER IN MY NAME, THERE AM I IN THE
MIDST OF THEM."
Matthew 18.18-20

We have seen how the church ought to bind what
God wishes to bind and to loose what God wishes to loose. How, though, is the church actually to bind and to loose? "Again I say unto you, that if two of you shall agree on earth as touching anything that they shall ask, it shall be done for them of my Father who is in heaven" (verse 19). The preceding verse (verse 18) lays stress upon both the earth and heaven, but so does this verse. Verse 18 speaks of heaven binding or loosing whatever the earth

23 神前有能

binds or looses, but so too does verse 19, which says that the heavenly Father will do whatever the earth asks for. Please note that what the Lord Jesus emphasizes here is not simply an agreeing in the asking of any one thing, rather is it an agreeing on earth as touching everything whatever they shall ask. He does not mean to say that two persons agree on earth touching a certain thing and they then ask for it; no, the Lord Jesus is saying that if you agree on *everything,** then whatever *particular* point you shall ask for, it shall be done for them of His Father who is in heaven. This is the oneness of the body, or may it be said, the oneness in the Holy Spirit.

If a person's flesh has not been dealt with, he will consider himself a superman since, in his view, heaven must hear him. No, if you are not in the oneness of the Holy Spirit, nor are praying in the harmony of the Holy Spirit, just see whether heaven will hear you at all. You may pray, but heaven will not bind what you bind nor loose what you loose. For this is not something you are capable of doing by yourself. If you think you *can* do it alone, you plainly think foolishly. For what the Lord declares is this: "If two of you shall agree on earth as touching anything that they shall ask, it

---

* *The meaning here is not the literal concurrence on everything between two persons, but the harmony in the Holy Spirit as described by the author in the paragraphs that follow.—Translator*

shall be done for them of my Father who is in heaven."This means should two of you be harmonious concerning any and every matter—being just as harmonious as is music— then whatever item you shall ask for, it shall be done for you by the heavenly Father. To pray such prayer requires the work of the Holy Spirit in the persons who pray. That is to say, I as one brother am brought by God to a place where I deny all my desires and will (want) only what the Lord wants and another brother is likewise brought by the Holy Spirit to that place of denying all his desires and wanting only what the Lord wills. I and he, he and I, are both brought to a place where there is such harmony as is true in music. And then, whatever we shall ask, God in heaven will perform for us.

Brethren, do not fancy that simply so long as we concur on an item for prayer (without a prior harmony in the Holy Spirit), our prayer will be heard. Not so. People with the same idea often have many conflicts. Merely having the same aim does not guarantee the absence of discord. Two may both want to preach the gospel, but they may still quar- rel between themselves. Two may completely desire to help others, nevertheless they rub against one another. Sameness in purpose does not necessarily mean harmony. We ought to realize that there is no possibility of harmony in the flesh.

23　　　　　神前有能

Only when our natural life is dealt with by the Lord and we begin to live in the Holy Spirit—I living in Christ as well as you living in Christ—will we ever have harmony, and will we ever then be able to pray with one accord on a given matter.

Here then are two facets of one thing: the first is a being in harmony about everything, the second is a praying for anything. We need to be brought by God to such a place as this. Apart from the body of Christ there is no place where Christian harmony may be found. Harmony is in the body of Christ. Only there is there the absence of strife, only there is there harmony. If our natural life is dealt with by the Lord and we are brought to really know what the body of Christ is, then are we in harmony and our prayer together will be in harmony too. Because we stand on the ground of harmony, we also agree on any particular matter. Since what we see is harmonious, we are qualified to be the mouthpiece of God's will. Brothers and sisters, when you are praying for a certain matter, if you have a different opinion be careful lest you err. Only when the whole church gathers together and agrees on that matter do we find that heaven wills to do it. For this reason, therefore, let us trust the church.

Keep in mind that prayer is not the first thing to be done. Prayer only follows on the heels of harmony. If the church

神前有能　　　　　　　**23**

desires to have such a ministry of prayer on earth, each and every brother and sister must learn to deny the life of the flesh before the Lord, else the church will not be effective. The word which the Lord Jesus gives us here is most wonderful. He does not say that if you ask in His name the Father will hear you; nor does the Lord say that He will pray for them that the Father may answer. Instead, He declares: "If two of you shall agree on earth as touching anything that they shall ask, it shall be done for them of my Father who is in heaven." Oh! If we really agree, the gate of heaven shall be opened!

"For where two or three are gathered together in my name, there am I in the midst of them" (v.20). Here is the third principle, and the most profound of them too. In verse 18 we have a principle, in verse 19 another principle, and verse 20 still another. The principle given in verse 20 is broader than that of verse 19. Why does verse 19 say that "if two of you shall agree on earth as touching anything that they shall ask, it shall be done for them of my Father who is in heaven"? The answer is given in verse 20: "For where two or three are gathered together in my name, there am I in the midst of them." Why is there such great power on earth? Why does praying in harmony have such tremendous effect? What gives the praying in harmony of two or three persons this much power? It is because whenever we are called to gather together in the name of the Lord the presence of the Lord Himself is there. This is the cause of agreement. Verse 18 speaks of the relation between earth and heaven; verse 19, of the prayer of harmony on earth; verse 20, of the cause for such harmony.

It is the Lord who is directing everything. Since He is here directing, enlightening, speaking and revealing, therefore what things soever shall be bound on earth shall also be bound in heaven and what things soever shall be loosed on earth shall be loosed in heaven. It is all because the Lord is here working together with His church.

We consequently need to learn how to deny ourselves before the Lord. Each time He calls us to gather together we should be turned to His name, for His name is higher than all other names. All idols must be smashed. Thus shall He lead us.

Brothers and sisters, this is not feeling nor theory, but fact. If the church is normal, then after each gathering she knows whether the Lord is here. When the Lord is present, the church is rich and strong. During such time she can either bind or loose. But if the Lord is not in the midst, she can do nothing. Only the church possesses such power; the individual simply does not have it within him.

神前有能   **23**

Notes and Meditations from:

Day Twenty Three – *Harmony in the Holy Spirit*

24

神前有能

Authoritative Prayer

"HAVE FAITH IN GOD."
Mark 11.23

In the Bible can be found a kind of prayer which is the highest and the most spiritual, yet few people notice or offer up such utterance. What is it? It is "authoritative prayer". We know prayer of praise, prayer of thanksgiving, prayer of asking, and prayer of intercession, but we know very little of prayer of authority. Authoritative prayer is that which occupies a most significant place in the Word. It signifies authority, even the command of authority.

Now if we desire to be men and women of prayer, we must learn this authoritative kind. It is the type of prayer which the Lord refers to in Matthew 18.18—"What things soever ye shall bind on earth shall be bound in heaven; and what things soever ye shall loose on earth shall be loosed in heaven." Here is loosing as well as binding prayer. The movement of heaven follows the movement of the earth. Heaven listens to the words on earth and acts on the earth's command. Whatsoever is bound on earth shall be bound in heaven; and whatsoever is loosed on earth shall be loosed in heaven. It is not an ask-

24 神前有能

ing on earth but a binding on earth; it is not an asking on earth but a loosing on earth. And this is authoritative prayer.

Such an expression can be found in Isaiah 45.11, which runs: "Command ye me." How do we dare to command God? Is not this too preposterous? too presumptuous? But this is what God Himself says. Doubtless we should not in the least allow the flesh to come in here. Nevertheless we are hereby shown that there is a kind of commanding prayer. According to God's viewpoint we may command Him. Such utterance needs to be learned specifically by all students of prayer.

In our day where does such prayer of command find its origin with the Christian? It has its origin at the ascension of the Lord. Ascension is very much related to the Christian life. What is the relationship? Ascension gives us victory. Just as the death of Christ solves our old creation in Adam, and resurrection leads us into the new creation, so ascension gives us a new position in the face of Satan. This is not a new position before God, for such position is obtained by the resurrection of the Lord. Nonetheless, our new position before Satan is secured through the ascension of Christ.

Note these words from Ephesians: "And made him [Christ] to sit at his right hand in the heavenly places, far above all rule, and authority, and power, and dominion, and every name that is named, not only in this world, but also in that which is to come: and he put all things in subjection under his feet" (1.20-22a). When Christ ascends to heaven He opens a way to heaven, so that henceforth His church may also ascend from earth to heaven. We know our spiritual foe dwells in the air; but today Christ is already ascended to heaven. A new way is therefore opened up from earth to heaven. This way was formerly blocked by Satan, but now Christ has opened it up. Christ is now far above all rule and authority and power and dominion and every name that is named, not only in this world, but also in that which is to come. This is the current position of Christ. In other words, God has caused Satan and all his subordinates to be subject to Christ; yea, He has put all things in subjection under His feet.

The significance of ascension is quite different from that of death and resurrection. While the latter is wholly for the sake of redemption, the former is for warfare—namely, to execute what His death and resurrection have accomplished. Ascension makes manifest a new position. Thank God, for we are told that He has "raised us up with him, and made us to sit with him in the heavenly places, in Christ Jesus" (Ephesians 2.6).

Authoritative prayer is based on this heavenly position.

24 神前有能

Because the church is with Christ in the heavenly places, she may pray the prayer of authority.

What is authoritative prayer? Simply explained, it is the type of prayer mentioned in Mark 11. In order to see the truth clearly let us read verses 23 and 24 carefully. Verse 24 begins with "therefore"—a connective term. So that the words in verse 24 are joined to those in verse 23. Since verse 24 speaks about prayer, verse 23 must also refer to prayer. What appears strange here is that in verse 23 it does not seem like an ordinary prayer. It does not say to God: "O God, please take up this mountain and cast it into the sea." What instead does it actually say? It reads there: "Whosoever shall say unto this mountain, Be thou taken up and cast into the sea."

What would the type of prayer be which is so often formed in our mind? We think in praying to God that it should always be: "O God, will You please take up this mountain and cast it into the sea?" But the Lord is talking about something quite different. He does not exhort us to speak to God, He instructs us to speak to the mountain. Not a speaking to God, but a speaking directly to the mountain—"Be thou taken up and cast into the sea." Lest we might not consider this as prayer, the Lord immediately explains in verse 24 that this is indeed prayer. Here is a word which is not directed to

神前有能

God, and yet it too is prayer. To speak to the mountain and command it to be cast into the sea is unquestionably a prayer. And this is authoritative in nature. For authoritative prayer is not asking God to do something but using God's authority to deal directly with problems, to get rid of all that needs to be got rid of. Such prayer needs to be learned by each and every overcomer. All who overcome must learn to speak to the mountain.

To ask God to remove the mountain and to command the mountain itself to move are two entirely opposite things. To come to God and ask Him to work is one thing, to directly command the mountain to move away is quite another thing. Such word of command is often neglected by us. It is very rare that we take the authority of God and speak directly to the difficulty, saying: "In the name of the Lord Jesus I ask you to leave me" or "I will not allow you to remain in my life." Authoritative prayer is for you to speak to whatever hinders you: "Depart from me." You will speak to your temper thusly: "Depart from me"; you will speak to your sickness as follows: "Depart from me, for by the resurrection life of the Lord I will get up." Not a speaking to God here, but a speaking directly to the mountain of hindrance, declaring: "Be thou taken up and cast into the sea." Now this is authoritative prayer.

24 神前有能

Oftentimes we speak to the mountains casually; such speaking will not be effective since we do not even know God's will. But if we are clear before God as to what His desire is and doubt not, we may boldly address the mountain, saying, "Be thou taken up and cast into the sea", and it shall in fact be done. Here the Lord appoints us to be those who give command. We command what God has already commanded—and this is the prayer of authority.

Hence authoritative prayer is not asking God directly, it is applying God's authority directly upon the difficulty. We each have our mountain. It may not be the same size nor perhaps of the same kind. As a rule, though, whatever blocks you in your spiritual course is something you may command to depart from you. This is authoritative prayer.

Only those who know authoritative prayer know what prayer really is. The principal work of overcomers is to bring the authority of the heavenly throne down to earth. Today there is only one throne—God's throne; He alone rules and reigns far above all. To share in that authority, there must be prayer. How necessary is prayer. That which can move the throne can move anything and everything. We need to see that Christ has ascended to heaven far above all and that all things are put in subjection under His feet. Thus will we be

神前有能　　24

able to use this throne-authority to govern all things. All of us must learn this authoritative prayer.

NOTES AND MEDITATIONS FROM:
DAY TWENTY FOUR – *Authoritative Prayer*

25

神前有能

Binding And Loosing

"CONCERNING THE WORKS OF MY HANDS, COMMAND YE ME."
Isaiah 45.11

Authoritative prayer may be divided into two sides: one side is the binding, the other side is the loosing. What things soever are bound on earth shall also be bound in heaven; and what things soever are loosed on earth shall also be loosed in heaven. What is done on earth shall also be done in heaven. This is Matthew 18.18. Verse 19 continues with prayer. So that the loosing as well as the binding are done through prayer. Loosing prayer and binding prayer are both authoritative prayers. Ordinary prayer will be asking God to bind and loose, but authoritative prayer is using authority to bind and loose by us. God so binds because the church has already bound; God so looses because the church has already loosed. God has given authority to the church; He will do whatever the church by that authority says.

Let us first discuss binding prayer. Many people and many things need to be bound. A brother is too talkative. He needs to be bound. You may go to God and pray: "O God, do not allow this brother to talk so much. Bind him that he may not do so." Thus will *you* bind him, but also *God* will bind him in heaven, so that he becomes less talkative. Or people may interrupt your prayer or your study of the Bible. Such people may be your wife or your husband, your children or your friends. You may use authority to utter binding prayer concerning these people who frequently interrupt you. You may say to God; "O God, bind them that they may not do anything to interrupt."

In a meeting some brother may say things which ought not to be said, may quote improper Scriptures, or may choose inappropriate hymns. Such a person needs to be bound. You may say: "Lord, So-and-so often errs; do not allow him to do these things any more." By so binding, you will see that God shall also bind him up. Sometimes some people will disturb the peace of the meeting—perhaps by talking, or crying, or walking to and fro. Such activities often occur in a meeting. And those who disturb are usually the same few people. These individuals and their acts need naturally to be bound. Therefore you say: "God, we notice that these people always disturb the meeting. Bind them and do not allow them to disturb." You shall see that if there are two or three on earth binding, God will also bind in heaven.

Not only all these disturbances need to be bound, but many of the works of the demons must be bound too. Each time the gospel is preached or testimony is given, the devil will be at work in human minds, whispering many words to them and injecting many ugly thoughts into them. Here the church must bind these evil spirits, forbidding them to whisper and to work. You should declare: "Lord, bind all the works of the evil spirits." If you on earth bind them, they shall likewise be bound in heaven.

The other side of authoritative prayer is loosing prayer. What needs to be loosed? Let us illustrate this concretely. Many timid brothers dare not open their mouths in the meeting. They are afraid of witnessing, or of seeing people. We must ask God to release such brothers from the bondage that is upon them. Sometimes we may perhaps exhort them with a few words; but at many other times we need not say anything to them; instead we approach the throne for its control over the situation. There are people who really should come out and serve the Lord, nonetheless they are bound either by occupation, or affairs of family, or unbelieving mates, or outward circumstance. They may be bound by all kinds of bondages. But we can ask the Lord to loose them that they may step out to witness for the Lord. Brethren, are we aware of the need of authoritative prayer? Do we really see its urgency?

25　　　　神前有能

As to the matter of money, it too should be loosed through our prayer. Satan often tightens the pocket of man. Sometimes we should ask God to release the money that His work may not suffer due to financial lack.

Truth also needs to be released. We should frequently pray: "O Lord, release your truth." Many truths are so bound that they are not proclaimed; many truths are proclaimed but few hear and understand. For this reason, we should ask God to release His truth that it may get through to His children. In many places, truth seems to be barred from entrance; there appears to be no possibility for people to receive it. How we must ask God to release the truth that many churches under bondage may be released and many places which are closed may be opened up. The Lord alone knows how to send the truth to closed places. As we pray with authority, the Lord shall send in the truth. Let us therefore be alert to the many things which must be loosed through authoritative prayer.

We should pay special attention to binding prayer and loosing prayer. Many things need to be bound; many things must be loosed. Here we do not beg; rather, we use authority to bind and to loose. May God be gracious to us that we all may learn how to use authority in prayer. Not only must we learn how to pray, we must also know what is the victory

神前有能　　　　　　　　　　25

of Christ. In the victory of Christ we release, in the victory of Christ we bind. We will bind all the things that are contrary to God's will. Authoritative prayer is heaven's rule on earth or the using of heaven's authority on earth.

Today we are but sojourners on the earth; in reality each of us is a heavenly person, therefore we have heavenly authority. Hence every one who is called by the name of the Lord is, on earth, a representative of the Lord. We are God's ambassadors. We have His life and have been delivered out of the power of darkness and been translated into the kingdom of the Son of God's love; consequently, we possess heavenly authority. At all times and in all places we hold the authority of heaven. We may control earthly affairs by means of heaven. May God give us grace that we may truly be prayer warriors for the Lord's sake, exercising His authority as overcomers that the victory of Christ may be manifested.

Finally, a serious warning is in order here; which is, that we must ourselves be subject to the authority of God. Except we are in subjection to God's authority we cannot exercise authoritative prayer. We should be subject not only to God's authority positionally but also in our daily life and practices; otherwise we will not have authoritative prayer.

神前有能

The Bible, moreover, reveals a close relationship between prayer, fasting, and authority. Prayer bespeaks our desire for God; while fasting illustrates our self-denial. The first privilege God granted to man was food. God gave Adam food before giving him anything else. So that fasting signifies a denial of man's first legal right. Many Christians fast without actually denying self; and thus their fast is not accepted as being such. The Pharisees fasted on the one hand but extorted on the other. If they had really fasted, they would have repaid what they had extorted. Since prayer is a desiring after God and fasting is a denying of self, faith will instantly be sparked when these two factors are joined. And then with faith, there is authority to cast out demons. Now if we desire after God yet refuse to deny self, we will not have faith and so neither will we have authority. But if we have both a desire for God and a denial of self, we shall instantly possess both faith and authority. We may quickly generate the prayer of faith, even unto authoritative prayer. And keep in mind that authoritative prayer is the most spiritual as well as the most important of prayers.

25

NOTES AND MEDITATIONS FROM:

DAY TWENTY FIVE – *Binding And Loosing*

Prayer Warfare

"FOR THE WORKS OF OUR WARFARE ARE NOT FLESHLY, BUT POWERFUL ACCORDING TO GOD TO THE OVERTHROW OF STRONGHOLDS."
2 Corinthians 10.4 Darby

D o we now see what God has done for us? In the first chapter of Ephesians we are told that Christ is ascended to heaven, far above all rule and authority and power and dominion and every name that is named, not only in this world, but also in that which is to come. In the second chapter it continues by telling us that we are now seated with Him in the heavenly places. This is the same as telling us that the *church* is also far above all rule and authority and power and dominion and every name that is named, not only in this world, but also in that which is to come. Thank God, this is a fact. As Christ is now in heaven far above all, so the church today too is far above all. As the Lord is far above all spiritual foes, so is the church far above all spiritual foes. As all spiritual foes are surpassed by the Lord at His ascension, so too are these spiritual foes surpassed by the church which has ascended with the Lord. Accordingly, all spiritual foes are put in subjection under the feet of the church.

26

神前有能

Let us notice the connection between Ephesians 1, 2 and 6. Chapter 1 shows us our position in Christ; Chapter 2, the position of the church in Christ; and Chapter 6, what the church should do now that she has entered upon that position in Christ. Chapter 1 speaks of Christ in heaven; Chapter 2, of the church seated with Christ in the heavenly places; and Chapter 6, of spiritual warfare. God has made the church to sit with Christ in the heavenly places that she may not only sit there but also stand. So that when Chapter 2 mentions "sit", Chapter 6 says "stand", which signifies standing in the heavenly position: "Against the principalities, against the powers, against the world-rulers of this darkness, against the spiritual hosts of wickedness in the heavenly places . . . and, having done all, to stand" (6.12,13). Since our warfare is against the spiritual hosts of wickedness, it is a spiritual warfare.

"With all prayer and supplication praying at all seasons in the Spirit, and watching thereunto in all perseverance and supplication for all the saints, and on my behalf. . . . " (Ephesians 6.18,19a). This is the prayer of spiritual warfare. This kind of prayer is different from the ordinary kind. The ordinary kind is praying from earth to heaven, but the kind of prayer here spoken of is a standing in the heavenly position and praying from heaven down to earth. Authoritative prayer begins in heaven and ends on earth. In short, authoritative prayer is a praying from heaven to earth.

All who know how to pray know what is meant by praying upward and what is meant by praying downward. If a person has never learned how to pray downward, he has yet to discover authoritative prayer. In spiritual warfare this kind of praying downward is exceedingly important. What is praying downward? It is standing upon the heavenly position Christ has given us and using authority to resist all the works of Satan by commanding that whatever God has commanded must be done. Suppose, for example, that we are praying for a particular matter. After we have seen what the will of God is and have really ascertained what God has ordered, we should then not pray: "O God, I ask You to do this thing"; on the contrary, we should pray: "God, You must do this thing, it must be done in this way. God, this thing must so be accomplished." This is commanding prayer—prayer of authority.

The meaning of "amen" is not "let it be so" but "thus shall it be". When I say amen to your prayer I am affirming that thus shall the matter be, that what you pray shall so be accomplished. This is the prayer of command, which comes out of faith. The reason we may so pray is because we have the heavenly position. We are brought into this heavenly position when Christ ascends to heaven. As Christ is in heaven so we too are in heaven, just as when Christ died and was resurrected, we also died and were resurrected. We ought to see the heavenly position of the church. Satan commences his work by causing us if he can to lose our heavenly position. For the heavenly is the position of victory. As long as we *stand* in that position, we are victorious. But if by Satan we are dragged down from heaven, we are defeated.

All victories are gained by standing in the heavenly, triumphant position. Satan will tempt you, saying, "You are on earth"; and you are defeated indeed if you answer, "I am on earth." He will use such defeat to trouble you, causing you to consider yourself as truly on earth. But if you stand and reply: "As Christ is in heaven, so I am in heaven", you lay hold of your heavenly position and are victorious. Hence standing in position is of great importance.

If God is to have a company of overcomers there must be prayer warfare. We need to battle with Satan not only when we encounter something but also when things happen around us. We must control them through the throne. No one can be an overcomer without being a prayer warrior. For one to be truly an overcomer before God he must learn to pray the prayer of authority.

神前有能

The church is able to control hell by using authoritative prayer. Since Christ is far above all and the head of the church, the church is well able to control evil spirits and all who belong to Satan. How could she ever exist on earth if she were not given the authority to control evil spirits—if the Lord has not given such authority to her? She lives because she has the authority over all Satanic forces. Those who are spiritual know we may use authoritative prayer against evil spirits. We may cast out demons in the name of the Lord; we may contain the secret activities of the evil spirits by prayer.

The wiles of Satan are manifold: his evil spirits not only possess people in the open, he also works secretly in many ways. At times he works in the mind of man, therein injecting many evil thoughts such as suspicion, terror, disbelief, disappointment, imagination, or distortion so as to deceive and upset. At other times he steals away man's words and creates a certain thought which he presses into another person's mind that he may succeed in dividing and disturbing. We must use prayer to overcome all the various activities of the evil spirits. In meetings, at prayers, or in conversations we may first declare: "Lord, drive away all evil spirits and forbid them to have any activity in this place."

It is a fact that all the evil spirits are put in subjection under

神前有能

the feet of the church. If the church uses authority to pray, even the evil spirits will be subject to her. Authoritative prayer is not like any ordinary asking; it is the exercising of authority to command. Authoritative utterance is the prayer of command, saying, "Lord, I am willing", "Lord, I am not willing", "Lord, I will", "Lord, I will not", "Lord, I am determined to hear this", "Lord, I will not let this pass", or "Lord, only Your will be done, I want nothing else". When we use this authority, our prayer will achieve its goal. If there were more people in the church learning to pray in this manner, many more problems in the church would be easily solved. We should rule and manage the affairs of the church through prayer.

We must see that Christ has already ascended to heaven; otherwise, we have no power to direct. Christ is now the head of all things, and all things are put in subjection under His feet. He is the head over all things to the church. He becomes the head of all things for the sake of the church. And as Christ is head over all things to the church, all things must necessarily be under the church. We need to take spiritual note of this.

神前有能 **26**

NOTES AND MEDITATIONS FROM:

DAY TWENTY SIX – *Prayer Warfare*

27 神前有能

Prayer Against Our Enemy

"BE SUBJECT THEREFORE UNTO GOD; BUT RESIST THE DEVIL, AND HE WILL FLEE FROM YOU."

James 4.7

The most important thing before us now is to identify the enemy. We should know for sure who is our adversary, who it is that causes us much suffering. How frequently we account our sufferings to be from men. But the Bible tells us that "our wrestling is not against flesh and blood, but against the principalities, against the powers, against the world rulers of this darkness, against the spiritual hosts of wickedness in the heavenly places" (Ephesians 6.12). Hence every time we suffer from the hand of man, we need to remember that behind flesh and blood Satan and his powers of darkness can very well be there directing everything. We should have the necessary spiritual insight to discern the work of God from the maneuver of Satan at the back of everything. We should distinguish what is natural and what is supernatural. We should be so inwardly exercised as to gain knowledge of the spiritual realm so that none of Satan's hidden work can escape our observation.

Such being the case, shall we not recognize that what we

神前有能

usually consider to be incidental and natural happenings may involve the works of the enemy behind the scenes? We shall readily see that Satan is really trying to frustrate us at every turn and oppress us in all things. What a pity we have suffered so much from him in the past without knowing that it was he who made us suffer. Now part of the most urgent work of ours today is to generate a heart of hatred towards Satan for his cruelty. We do not need to be fearful lest our enmity towards Satan becomes too deep. Before there is the possibility of our overcoming we must maintain in our heart a hostile attitude towards him, no longer willing to subject ourselves to his oppression. We ought to understand that what we have suffered at Satan's hands is a real grievance which must be avenged. He has no right to harass us, yet he does it anyway. This is indeed an injustice, a grievance which cannot remain unavenged.

After the widow has suffered much, she comes to the judge asking for justice (see Luke 18.1-8). This is something we ought to learn to do. We do not come to earthly judges, imploring them to act for us. No, we ask our judge who is none other than our Father God in heaven. The weapons of our warfare are not of the flesh (2 Corinthians 10.4), therefore we will not employ any earthly or fleshly means against the instruments of flesh and blood utilized by Satan. Quite

神前有能　　　　　　　27

the contrary, instead of showing impatience, anger or even
hostility towards them, we should pity them for they are but
the instruments of Satan. Let us see that in spiritual warfare
the weapons of flesh are utterly useless. They are not only
useless, but whoever uses them will without fail be overcome by Satan.

Spiritual weapons are of many kinds as we find recorded in
Ephesians 6. The most effective among these weapons is
prayer, mentioned in verse 18. True, we are without strength
and therefore unable to avenge ourselves of our adversary. Yet
we may pray to our God, asking him to avenge us. Prayer is
the best offensive weapon against our enemy. Through it we
may preserve our line of defense intact. Through prayer we
can also attack our enemy and inflict great loss on his plan,
work, and power. This widow realized that if she struggled
with her adversary by herself she would not prevail because
she, being a weak widow, could never withstand a powerful
rogue (villain) such as he. In the same way, if God's children
strive independently without relying, by means of prayer, on
God's power and backing to accuse the enemy and to ask
God for vindication, they too will be injured by fiery darts. In
this parable the Lord Jesus teaches us the best way to overcome the adversary, which is to pray day and night to God—
asking Him to avenge us of our enemy by judging him.

27

神前有能

The Bible gives us many helps in this matter of praying against Satan. We will here examine a few of these passages so as to learn how to offer up such prayer.

We recall how in Genesis 3 God punished and cursed the devil after his first evil working. In that divine curse God plainly foretold that the head of the devil would be crushed by the Lord Jesus at the cross. Accordingly, whenever we suffer under the devil's hands we may take advantage of the punishment meted out to him by praying: "O God, curse Satan afresh so that he cannot do what he pleases. You have crushed him in the garden of Eden. I ask You to curse him anew, placing him again under the power of the cross so as to immobilize him." What the devil fears most is the curse of God. As soon as God curses, Satan dare not hurt us.

It is recorded in Mark 1 that when the Lord Jesus cast out demons He did not permit them to speak. Hence when Satan uses people to utter many words of misunderstanding or violence, we may ask the Lord to shut his mouth and not permit him to speak through them. Sometimes as we are preaching the gospel or teaching people, we may ask the Lord to forbid the devil to speak to our audience so as to induce them to doubt or to resist the Word of God. We remember the story of Daniel in the lions' den. One prayer is

神前有能　　　　　　　**27**

really quite effective:"O Lord, shut the lion's mouth; do not allow him to hurt Your own people."

Matthew 12 furnishes us with another good word on prayer from the Lord:"How can one enter into the house of the strong man, and spoil his goods, except he first bind the strong man? and then he will spoil his house" (v.29). We know that the strong man to whom the Lord refers is Satan. In order to overcome Satan we must first bind him, thus immobilizing him. We ourselves, of course, do not have the strength to bind the strong man and cause him to lose his freedom in resisting our works. But we can pray. In our prayer we may ask God to bind Satan and render him powerless. Each time we begin a work, if we first bind Satan in prayer our victory is assured. We ought always to pray:"O Lord, bind the strong man."

"To this end was the Son of God manifested, that he might destroy the works of the devil" (1 John 3.8). As soon as we discern a work of the devil, we can pray as follows:"O God, Your Son was manifested to destroy the works of the devil. How we thank You, for He has destroyed the devil's works on the cross. But the devil is now again working. Please destroy his work in us, destroy his manipulation over our work, destroy his devices in our environment, and destroy all his

27 神前有能

works."When we pray, we may pray according to the current situation in which we find ourselves. If we notice that Satan is working in us or family or work or school or nation, we can ask God to destroy his work in that particular area.

Jude records the word which Michael the archangel declared to Satan:"The Lord rebuke thee" (v.9). After that word was spoken Satan did not dare resist anymore. We may therefore use this same word in our prayer against him. We ask the Lord to rebuke the enemy. We ought to know that the Lord hearkens to such prayer. If we ask Him to rebuke, He will rebuke. We must also believe that after the Lord has rebuked Satan, the enemy is no longer able to withstand, for he is afraid of the Lord's rebuke. When our Lord rebuked the wind and the sea, these elements listened to Him and instantly the wind ceased and the sea became calm. His rebuke produces the same effect on Satan.

神前有能 27

NOTES AND MEDITATIONS FROM:

DAY TWENTY SEVEN – *Prayer Against Our Enemy*

28

神前有能

Prayer and God's Work

"I HAVE SET WATCHMEN UPON THY WALLS, O JERUSALEM, THEY
SHALL NEVER HOLD THEIR PEACE DAY OR NIGHT; YE THAT ARE
JEHOVAH'S REMEMBRANCERS, TAKE YE NO REST, AND GIVE HIM NO
REST, TILL HE ESTABLISH, AND TILL HE MAKE JERUSALEM A PRAISE
IN THE EARTH."

Isaiah 62.6,7

When God works, He does so with specific law and definite principle. Even though He could do whatever pleases Him, yet He never acts carelessly. He always performs according to His determinate law and principle. Unquestionably He can transcend all these laws and principles, for He is God and is quite capable of acting according to His own pleasure. Nonetheless, we discover a most marvelous fact in the Bible; which is, that in spite of His exceeding greatness and His ability to operate according to His will, God ever acts along the line of the law or principle which He has laid down. It seems as though He deliberately puts Himself under the law to be controlled by His own law.

Now then, what is the principle of God's working? God's working has a primal (basic) principle behind it, which is,

神前有能

that He wants man to pray, that He desires man to cooperate with Him through prayer.

There was once a Christian who well knew how to pray. He declared this, that all spiritual works include four steps: The first step is that God conceives a thought, which is His will: The second step is that God reveals this will to His children through the Holy Spirit, causing them to know that He has a will, a plan, a demand and expectation: The third step is that God's children return His will by praying to Him, for prayer is responding to God's will—if our heart is wholly one with His heart, we will naturally voice in our prayer what He intends to do: And the fourth step is that God will accomplish this very thing.

Here we are concerned not with the first step nor with the second, but with the third step—how we are to return God's will by praying to Him. Please notice the word "return". All prayers with worth possess this element of return in them. If our prayer is only for the purpose of accomplishing our plan and expectations it does not have much value in the spiritual realm. Prayer must originate from God and be responded to by us. Such alone is meaningful prayer, since God's *work* is controlled by such prayer. How many things the Lord indeed desires to do, yet He does not perform them because His

神前有能

people do not pray. He will wait until men agree with Him, and then He will work. This is a great principle in God's working, and it constitutes one of the most important principles to be found in the Bible.

The word in Ezekiel 36.37 is quite surprising. The Lord says He has a purpose, which is, that He will increase the house of Israel with men like a flock. This is the determinate will of God. What He ordains He will perform. Nevertheless, He will not accomplish it instantly but will wait awhile. What is the reason for the waiting? The Lord says, "For this, moreover, will I be inquired of by the house of Israel, to do it for them." He has decided to increase the house of Israel with men, but He must wait till the children of Israel inquire of Him about the matter. Let us see that even if He Himself has resolved to perform certain things He will not do so immediately. He will wait until men show their agreement before He proceeds. Each time He works He never goes ahead immediately simply because He has His will; no, He will wait, if necessary, for His people to express their agreement in prayer before He does act. This assuredly is a most amazing phenomenon.

Let us always be mindful of this truth, that all spiritual works are decided by God and desired by His children—all are initiated by God and approved by His children. This is a great principle in spiritual work. "For this, moreover, will I be inquired of by the house of Israel," says the Lord. His work awaits the inquiring of the children of Israel. And one day the Israelites really inquired, and without delay He performed it for them.

Do we see this principle of God's work? After He has initiated something, He pauses in its execution until we pray. Since the time of the founding of the church, there is nothing God does on earth without the prayer of His children. From the moment He has His children, He does everything according to the prayer of His own. He puts everything in their prayer. We do not know why He acts in such a way; but we do know that this is a fact. God is willing to condescend Himself to such a position of taking delight in fulfilling His will through His children.

There is another illustration of this in Isaiah 62: "I have set watchmen upon thy walls, O Jerusalem; they shall never hold their peace day or night: ye that are Jehovah's remembrancers, take ye no rest, and give him no rest, till he establish, and till he make Jerusalem a praise in the earth" (v.6,7). God intends to make Jerusalem a praise in the earth. How does He realize it? He sets watchmen upon its walls that they may cry to Him. How should they cry? "Take ye no rest, and give him no rest"—we are to cry to Him unceasingly and give Him no rest. We keep on praying until He accomplishes His work. Although the Lord has already willed to make Jerusalem a praise in the earth, He nonetheless sets watchmen on its walls. By their prayer will He perform. He urges them not to pray just once, but to pray without ceasing. Keep on praying till His will is done. In other words, the will of God is governed by the prayers of man. The Lord waits for us to pray. Let us understand clearly that as regards the *content* of God's will it is entirely decided by God Himself; we do not make, nor even participate in, the decision. Yet concerning the *doing* of His will it is governed by our prayer.

A brother once observed that God's will is like a train whereas our prayer is like the rails of a train. A train may travel to any place, except that it must run on rails. It has tremendous power to go east, west, south and north, but it can only run to places where rails have been laid. So that it is not because God has no power (He, like a train, *has* power, great power); but because He chooses to be governed by man's prayer, therefore all valuable prayers (like a train's rails) pave the way for God. Consequently, if we do not take up the responsibility of prayer, we will hinder the fulfillment of God's will.

神前有能

As we read through church history, we may notice that every great revival has always come from prayer. This shows us how prayer enables the Lord to do what He desires to do. We cannot ask Him to do what He does not want to do, though we may certainly *delay* what He wishes to do. God is absolute; therefore, we cannot change Him, neither can we force Him to do what He does not want to do, nor can we persuade Him *not* to do what He wants to do. Even so, when we are called to be the channel of His will we may doubtless block God's work if we do not cooperate with Him.

神前有能

28

NOTES AND MEDITATIONS FROM:

DAY TWENTY EIGHT – *Prayer and God's Work*

神前有能

DAY TWENTY NINE

Corporate Prayer

"IF MY PEOPLE, WHO ARE CALLED BY MY NAME, SHALL HUMBLE
THEMSELVES, AND PRAY, AND SEEK MY FACE, AND TURN FROM
THEIR WICKED WAYS; THEN WILL I HEAR FROM HEAVEN, AND WILL
FORGIVE THEIR SIN, AND WILL HEAL THEIR LAND."
2 Chronicles 7.14

Christianity is unique in that it is not individual but collective in nature. It stresses the assembling together of the saints. All other religions advocate individual piety; Christianity alone calls people to assemble. God's special grace falls on the gathering of believers.

Because of this, the Word of God commands us not to forsake assembling together. Even in the Old Testament, God ordained that the Jews should assemble; then He called them the congregation of the Lord. To be a congregation they had to assemble together. Thus in the Old Testament God already emphasized the gathering of His people. In the New Testament it becomes much clearer that men ought to assemble in order that they may receive His grace. The command of the Bible is, "not forsaking our own assembling together." No one can forsake such assembling without forfeiting grace. It is foolish to cease gathering with the saints.

29 神前有能

The Bible records many occasions of assembling together. While our Lord was on earth, He often met with His disciples. Though sometimes He conversed with them individually, yet He was more interested in gathering together with them. He gathered with them in boats, in homes, on top of mountains, and even inside a borrowed upper room on the night of His betrayal. After His resurrection, He met with them behind a closed door. Before the day of Pentecost, the disciples gathered with one accord and continued steadfastly in prayer. On the day of Pentecost, they were also all together in one place. Again, in Acts 2, we find that all who received the word and were baptized "continued stedfastly in the apostles' teaching and fellowship, in the breaking of bread and the prayers" (Acts 2.42). Later on, under persecution, they went to their own company where there was a gathering for prayer. When Peter was miraculously released from prison, he too went to a home where the people assembled in prayer. The epistles also command believers to not forsake assembling together. In Corinthians, special mention is made of the whole church coming together. No one who belongs to the church ought to keep himself away from such gatherings.

What is the meaning of the word "church" (more accurately, "assembly") in Greek? *Ek* means "out of," and *klesis* means "a

calling." *Ecclesia* means "the called-out ones assembled."
Today God has not only called out a people but He also
wants them to assemble together. If each one who is called
were to maintain his independence, there would be no
church. Thus we are shown the importance of assembling
together.

When we talk about the prayer of the church we are no less
concerned with private prayer nor sense any less the importance of personal prayer. Yet let us see that it is a rule in the
kingdom of God that what one person is unable to do in
certain respects is to be done through mutual and corporate
help. Especially in the matter of prayer, there is the need for
mutuality. All who follow the Lord closely frequently see the
need of praying with other believers. At times they feel the
inadequacy of their own prayer. Particularly in praying for
such a colossal subject as the kingdom of God, it requires
the strength of the whole church. "My house," says the Lord,
"shall be called a house of prayer" (Matthew 21.13). To this
we may add, "whose house are we" (Hebrews 3.6).

The body of Christ will deliver us from sect and sectarian-
ism; it will also save us from self and individualism. How sad
that the life principle of many is not the body but the individual self. We may discover this principle of individualism in

神前有能

many areas. For example, in a prayer meeting someone can only pray by himself, since he cannot pray with other people. His physical body may kneel together with others, yet his consciousness is circumscribed by his own self. When *he* prays, he wishes other people to listen to him; but when *others* pray, he will not listen to them. He has no inner response to another's prayer, and he is unable even to offer up an amen. His consciousness is disconnected from the consciousness of other people. Hence he prays *his* prayers and lets the others pray *their* prayers. There appears to be no relationship between his prayers and those of the others. When he comes to the meeting he seems to do so only for the sake of uttering whatever words are pent up within him, and thereafter feels that his job is done. He does not care what prayer burden or consciousness others present may have. This is the rule of individualism, not the principle of the body. In point of fact he has not seen the body, and thus he cannot cooperate with other people before God.

Oftentimes we need to learn fellowship in prayer, to learn fellowship in difficulties, to learn fellowship in seeking God's will, to learn fellowship concerning our future, and to learn fellowship regarding God's word. What fellowship means is that, knowing that I am inadequate in the matter of prayer, I seek out two or three others to pray with me. I by myself am incompetent in solving difficulties, hence I ask two or three brethren to deal with the situations together with me. Alone I am unable to know God's will, therefore I solicit the help of two or three others. I in myself am rather confused as to my future, consequently I request two or three brothers and sisters to fellowship and decide with me what my future should be. I cannot understand God's word alone, so now I study the Word of God with two or three brothers and sisters. In fellowship, I acknowledge my insufficiency and incompetency, and I also acknowledge my need of the body. I confess that I am limited and liable to make mistakes; for this I plead with those brothers and sisters who have spiritual discernment to help me (and not just ask those to help me who are affectionate towards me). I am inadequate, and hence I need the help of other brethren.

Because we are members of the body of Christ and members each in its part, we must seek how to help the body in gaining life and strength. In any gathering, even if we do not open our mouths, we may pray silently. Even though we may not speak, we can still look to God. This is body consciousness. If we have seen the body, we cannot say we are a person of no consequence. We will rather say: I am a member of the body, and hence I have a duty to perform. I have a word which I should speak, I have a prayer which I should utter. When I come to the meeting I must do whatever God wants me to do. I cannot afford to be a spectator. Such things as these are what we will say or do if we truly apprehend the body. And as we all function, the life of the entire gathering will swallow up all death. Many meetings fail to exhibit such power to overcome death for there are too many spectators.

神前有能

NOTES AND MEDITATIONS FROM:
DAY TWENTY NINE – *Prayer and God's Work*

Prayer Meeting (1)

"BUT FLEE YOUTHFUL LUSTS, AND FOLLOW AFTER RIGHTEOUSNESS, FAITH, LOVE, PEACE WITH THEM THAT CALL ON THE LORD OUT OF A PURE HEART."

2 Timothy 2.22

In order to see things done or to have the greatest power, the prayer meeting is most helpful. It can best measure spiritual strength. I hope many brothers and sisters will come, and that there will be many prayer burdens.

In a prayer meeting, as with all church meetings, assembly life not only helps a Christian's spiritual life, it also manifests the life of the body of Christ. If we overlook the gathering of the saints, we overlook the life together. And such is a great failure.

At a prayer meeting, things to be prayed for should be mentioned and explained. There ought not be too much speaking. Before we mention anything, let us ask ourselves if we have previously prayed for it at home. If it has not been prayed for at home, do not bring it out to deceive the brethren. Any matter which has not been prayed for at home shows neither need nor worth for prayer. This is a principle, a law. Whatever has not been prayed for personally has no need to be prayed for corporately. Only after it has been prayed for privately and a sense of personal inadequacy still lingers can it then be mentioned publicly in a prayer meeting.

Prayers offered in prayer meetings are heard most as well as least by God. Personal prayers are often heard, but corporate prayers are heard even more. People frequently use words and express sentiments in a prayer meeting which they do not use in their inner chamber. Oftentimes they pray with many words and on many things in a prayer meeting which they never do in their inner chamber. This ought not be so. Actually, whatever has not been a burden to pray for in the inner chamber should not be brought to the prayer meeting to be prayed for there. Prayer without burden ought not be uttered because it will not be heard by God. What prayer you feel inwardly is also felt by God. The power of prayer offered in a prayer meeting with burden and with one accord far exceeds individual prayer. If this were not true, there would be little point in having public prayer. Prayers offered with one heart without anything discordant existing between believers are most effective. God will surely hear such prayers. Hence the truth of the statement when we say that prayer is work.

Do not pray too long and too much. It is indeed true that

神前有能

prayer is like casting a net, yet it is not one person who casts the net. In case you sense something is left unprayed for, you should secretly ask God to raise up somebody else to pray for it. When I was in England, a Christian friend told me a story about a prayer meeting. There was a brother who prayed for many things. He felt he had prayed too long and ought to stop. Yet he also felt there were still many things which should be prayed for. On the one hand, he was afraid that if he ceased praying, nobody else would continue his prayer; on the other hand, he was apprehensive lest if he continued in prayer, he would occupy too much time. Still, out of consideration for other people, he decided to let some other brother pray. So he silently prayed within himself thus: I as an individual have prayed long enough in the meeting, please secure another brother, Lord, to continue my prayer. As he finished his public praying, somebody else actually continued his prayer and prayed for all the things which waited to be prayed for. So I would say that even if your thoughts are strong and good and many, you too should ask God to raise up other people at the same meeting to pray. God will attend to this request, for He is a living God. In a prayer meeting, we should give other people the opportunity to pray. Thus shall we pray with one accord and in life.

Sometimes God will use one among the brothers and sisters

to speak for them. All who are experienced in prayer know how very difficult it is to have suitable words to express a need. Often several persons have prayed for the same thing, and yet the burden is not discharged. So let us ask God to give us words to express our burden in prayer. Ask Him to raise up one among us who can express God's thought. At times there may be ten persons praying together for a certain matter, and all have prayed well. Nevertheless, the consensus among them still is that none has hit the mark. Suddenly one brother begins to pray; and as he prays, he hits the mark. Everybody senses that this is it, and all will say amen. This is praying in the Spirit. If there is no one who can express the inward need for all in a prayer meeting, that meeting is a failure. On the other hand, if people pray from 7:00 p.m. to 7:30 p.m. and have already arrived at the point of having had the burden discharged, all may go home for there is no need for further prayer. The words of the Holy Spirit are spoken by the Holy Spirit through man to express the mind of God. Such prayer is thorough and prevailing.

In 1926, I was severely ill in Foochow. My whole body turned purple. Three brothers and one sister came to my room to pray for me. The first one prayed with tears, yet I did not feel touched. The second one also prayed fervently, but I still did not sense anything. The third one was known as a prayer warrior, but his prayer too was of no avail. The fourth one to pray was that sister. As she opened her mouth, she prayed: "O God, people in hades cannot praise you, nor do you like them to praise you in hades" (cf. Psalm 115.17, 6.5; Isaiah 38.18). I instantly felt that this was it. Even before the prayer was ended, I knew I was well. The burden was lifted, and the sickness was healed. That very afternoon I got out of bed, and the next day I was on my way to travel for the Lord's work. Hence let us ask God to use us as a mouthpiece in the prayer meeting so that we may utter the words of the Holy Spirit to express the current burden and need of the brothers and sisters.

I will also mention what happened at the recently concluded conference. Our convocation began on the Lord's Day January 20. At the prayer meeting on the 17th, we prayed especially for this Victory Conference. Many brethren prayed fervently for many things, and I ardently responded with amens. However, there lingered a sense of need as if a burden had not been uttered. Later on, one brother opened his mouth and prayed: "O God, grant us good weather that it will not be too cold nor raining, nor snowing, and that we may also meet quietly." Everybody at the prayer meeting immediately felt touched, and the amens were louder than in the other prayers. Now before the conference commenced the weather had not been too good. Even in the evening of our prayer time (Thursday), it had been snowing. But on Friday before the conference, both rain and snow stopped. When did it rain again? The Thursday after our conference was concluded. During the whole time of the conference, it had not rained once. Furthermore, in the lane where we met, one family was holding a funeral. The day before the conference, on Saturday, they made a tremendous noise during their funeral observance. But on the second day they stopped. And only after our conference was over did they again begin to observe the funeral service with great noise. Had they done this during the conference, we would not have been able to meet quietly.

Hence in a prayer meeting, we need people to be the mouthpiece of the Holy Spirit. If we have such people, we will have no difficulty. For our difficulty is not knowing the need. Whenever the burden is lifted, the work is done.

神前有能

NOTES AND MEDITATIONS FROM:

DAY THIRTY – *Prayer Meeting (1)*

神前有能

Prayer Meeting (2)

"LET ALL THINGS BE DONE DECENTLY AND IN ORDER."
1 Corinthians 14.40

The prayer meeting is an important meeting. Each kind of meeting has its own particular characteristic. The testimony which God intends us to maintain on earth is to be fulfilled jointly by preaching the gospel, breaking bread, and praying together. Prayer meetings can be both difficult and easy. New believers need to learn about this kind of meeting.

1. WITH ONE ACCORD

A fundamental requirement for brothers and sisters praying together is to be of one accord. The Lord tells us in Matthew 18 that we must agree on earth. Before and on the day of Pentecost, the one hundred and twenty believers prayed with one accord (Acts 4.1-2). Therefore, the first condition of a prayer meeting is to be of one heart and one mind. How can people gather for prayer if each one has his own mind? The word "agree" in Matthew is most weighty. The Lord promises that, "If two of you shall agree on earth as touching anything

31

神前有能

that they shall ask, it shall be done for them . . ." (v. 19). This particular word in Greek is used in music to denote harmony. If a person is playing alone, there is no problem. But if three play together, one the piano, one the violin, and one the flute, should one of them play out of tune, the result is discord. Likewise our prayers should not be out of harmony. If we are able to agree with one another, God will hear whatever we ask. What we bind on earth shall be bound in heaven, and what we loose on earth shall be loosed in heaven. The basic condition is harmony. Therefore let us learn to be harmonious and not to pray each according to his own wish.

2. With Specific Requests

How can we achieve this goal of harmony? I observe that the greatest problem in many prayer meetings lies in too many requests. As long as there are too many subjects for which to pray, it is very difficult to arrive at harmony. We ourselves create disunity by having fifty or sixty prayer items. It becomes an all-inclusive meeting. We do not find such a situation in the Bible. What we do find there is praying for a specific matter. For example, the church prayed for Peter while he was in prison. We too should not pray for many things, but pray rather for one specific matter. It is easy to achieve agreement when there is only one topic. Too many items will make our prayers like a routine.

I believe the prayer meetings in many places require a drastic change. Let each prayer meeting be for just one thing. Perhaps we should pray for the unemployed brothers and sisters or for the sick or for the poor—one of these and nothing else. With one subject we can readily agree.

If there is yet time after we have finished praying for one matter, then we may mention another matter for prayer. We must do the work of prayer before God. The prayer meeting may be divided into two parts, in each part praying for one thing. To pray for two things at the same time makes it difficult for people to be of one accord. Do not therefore carelessly announce two items for prayer at the commencement. Let the responsible brother announce one thing at a time. I think the greatest need in a prayer meeting is to make the requests simple. The aim of prayer is to accomplish things, to get things done. It is not for social reasons or to please people; thus it cannot include everything.

The power of the specific prayer uttered in Acts 1 and 2 produced Pentecost. As the cross was the work accomplished by the Son of God, so Pentecost was the work accomplished through the prayer of God's children. How was it done? By praying with one accord. Let us, too, pray in that concentrated, not scattered, manner.

Everyone who attends a prayer meeting should come with the preparation of faith. If possible, the brothers and sisters should be told beforehand of the prayer request so that they may have a burden for it. First the sensing of the need, then the burden, and finally the asking.

3. IN REALITY

There is another basic need for the prayers at a prayer meeting, and that is, reality, or genuineness. According to my personal observation (I dare not exaggerate), I have reason to judge that one half of all the words uttered in a prayer meeting are false. The motive of many prayers is not that God may hear, but that man may approve. Whether God answers my prayer is not so important as long as it pleases men. As a consequence, prayers at the prayer meeting become pretentious and empty.

True prayer comes from the desire of the heart, not from the imagination of the mind. It expresses the feeling of the heart, so it arises from a deep longing within. For this reason prayer in the Old Testament was offered to God as incense.

神前有能

All Old Testament incense was made from trees. After the bark was cut, the tree oozed a kind of resin from which incense was manufactured. Hence prayer is not offering anything that might be at hand; it is the presenting of something dug out of the innermost heart. It resembles something that oozes out of wounds. Such prayers are quite different from the easygoing ones that many offer—prayers good to listen to, but very ordinary in content. Let us remember well that our prayers are for God to hear, not for pleasing the ears of brothers and sisters.

If the prayers of the prayer meetings lack reality, we frankly cannot expect the church to be strong. For the church to be strong, the prayer meetings must be strong. For the prayer meetings to be strong, all the prayers must be real. We cannot afford to let them be false, for God will never reward falsehood.

Prayer is not preaching, nor is it lecturing. It is asking before God. Therefore, do not use many words as if God were ignorant of the situation and in need of your detailed intelligence reports and arguments!

We pray because we have need; we pray because we have weakness. We come to receive spiritual supply and power.

31 神前有能

According to our sense of the measure of our need, to that extent do we pray in reality. If we sense no need, our prayer is bound to be unreal.

One of the fundamental causes of feigned prayer is that the one who prays simply cannot forget the other people present. Being always conscious of people, he easily becomes insincere in his prayer. Hence in a prayer meeting, he should remember that though on the one hand his prayer does represent the whole assembly, yet on the other hand he is alone with God, asking truly according to need.

The more definite the need, the more certain the prayer. You may remember the parable used by the Lord Jesus: a friend unexpectedly arrives and you have nothing to serve him. So you go to another friend to ask for bread. The need is very definite. "Ask, and it shall be given you; seek, and ye shall find; knock, and it shall be opened unto you," says the Lord Jesus (Matthew 7.7). You dare not be careless when there is a real need. The Lord promises that if you ask, you shall have it.

4. WITH CONCISENESS

Prayer needs to be concise as well as real. Almost all the prayers in the Bible are very concise. The so-called Lord's

神前有能

Prayer in Matthew 6 is quite short. The Lord's own prayer before His departure, recorded in John 17, seems to be long; yet it is much shorter than the prayers of many of God's children today. Even the prayer of the whole church found in Acts 4 is concise. The prayer in Ephesians 1 is a most important prayer, but it can easily be finished in less than five minutes.

Many times the longer the prayers are, the more pretentious and empty they become. Only two sentences are real; the rest are all added. Those two sentences are for God to hear; all the rest are for the ears of brothers and sisters. We should instruct young believers to pray briefly, telling them that if the older ones pray their long prayers, it is all right, but the young ones should not do so. As a matter of fact, long prayers can cause great damage to the church.

Once, when a sister prayed on and on, exhausting the patience of the whole assembly, Moody did a very wise thing by standing up and saying, "While our sister continues her prayer, let us sing a hymn." May none of us think that we can be careless during prayer meetings. If we really pray with one accord, unbelievers who happen to come in will have to acknowledge that these Christians do have something. Long prayers dissipate strength whereas concise prayers add strength to the meeting.

31

神前有能

The writer of the *Notes on the Pentateuch*, C. H. Mackintosh., spoke well when he said to please not use your prayer to ill-treat God's children. Many may not whip you with whips, but they beat you with prayers. You can hardly remain in your seat. Let God's children pray truly and concisely.

31

NOTES AND MEDITATIONS FROM:

DAY THIRTY ONE – *Prayer Meeting (2)*

Index of the Selected Excerpts

Index of the Selected Excerpts *(continued)*

Other Titles Available from Christian Fellowship Publishers

"Basic Lesson Series" by Watchman Nee

The Basic Lesson Series: Vol 1 - A Living Sacrifice

The Basic Lesson Series: Vol 2 - The Good Confession

The Basic Lesson Series: Vol 3 - Assembling Together

The Basic Lesson Series: Vol 4 - Not I But Christ

The Basic Lesson Series: Vol 5 - Do All to the Glory of God

The Basic Lesson Series: Vol 6 - Love One Another

Other Titles by Watchman Nee

Aids to "Revelation"

Back to the Cross

A Balanced Christian Life

The Better Covenant

The Body of Christ: A Reality

The Character of God's Workman

Christ the Sum of All Spirtual Things

The Church and the Work

Come, Lord Jesus

The Communion of the Holy Spirit

The Finest of the Wheat, vol 1

The Finest of the Wheat, vol 2

OTHER TITLES BY WATCHMAN NEE *(continued)*

THE SALVATION OF THE SOUL

THE SPIRIT OF JUDGMENT

THE SPIRIT OF THE GOSPEL

THE SPIRIT OF WISDOM AND REVELATION

SPIRITUAL AUTHORITY

SPIRITUAL KNOWLEDGE

THE SPIRITUAL MAN

SPIRITUAL REALITY OR OBSESSION

TAKE HEED

THE TESTIMONY OF GOD

THE COMPLETE WORKS OF WATCHMAN NEE (CD)

WHOM SHALL I SEND?

THE WORD OF THE CROSS

WORSHIP GOD

YE SEARCH THE SCRIPTURES

TITLES BY STEPHEN KAUNG

DISCIPLED TO CHRIST

SONGS OF DEGREES

THE SPLENDOR OF HIS WAYS